Anonymous

The Homes and Haunts of Thomas Carlyle

Anonymous

The Homes and Haunts of Thomas Carlyle

ISBN/EAN: 9783337059538

Printed in Europe, USA, Canada, Australia, Japan

Cover: Foto ©ninafisch / pixelio.de

More available books at **www.hansebooks.com**

THE HOMES AND HAUNTS

OF

THOMAS CARLYLE.

London:
"WESTMINSTER GAZETTE"
1895.
(All rights reserved.)

" We all love great men; love, venerate, and bow down submissive before great men: nay, can we honestly bow down to anything else?"—ON HEROES AND HERO WORSHIP.

PREFACE

"IN future years," wrote Carlyle's biographer, "in future centuries, strangers will come from distant lands, from America, from Australia, from New Zealand, from every isle or continent where the English language is spoken, to see the house where Carlyle was born, to see the green turf under which his dust is lying."

Mr. Froude's prediction has been verified at an earlier date than he assigned for it. It is only 14 years since Carlyle died, and already his birthplace has become a place of pilgrimage for men and women in all parts of the English-speaking world. The little house in Ecclefechan where the author of "Sartor Resartus" was born is visited by many hundreds of tourists every year. The other homes and haunts of his early life—the spots where he gazed on "those hues of gold and azure," and looked "at the fair illuminated letters with an eye for their gilding," are eagerly sought out by readers of "Heroes and Hero-Worship." The centenary of his birth has been the occasion of the purchase and dedication to the public for ever of the famous house in Chelsea, where the historian of the French Revolution, of Cromwell and of Friedrich did his life's work and lived out his life's drama.

This occasion seemed suitable to an attempt to collect together the scattered threads of interest thus suggested. To recall some of the more salient memories in the various Carlyle localities, to present some pictorial souvenirs of these, to furnish some kind of handbook to the *Homes and Haunts of Thomas Carlyle*: such are the objects of this little book which is now offered to the public as a contribution to the celebration of the Carlyle Centenary.

The greater part of the contents of the following pages is reprinted, though with large additions, from the columns of *The Westminster Gazette* and *The Westminster Budget*. But in the preparation of the present volume, we have been favoured with many valuable contributions, which we desire very gratefully to acknowledge. To Mr. G. G. Napier, M.A., we are specially indebted for permission to use several of the photographs which he prepared in connexion with his lecture on "The Vicinities of Carlyle." For permission to include a small reproduction of the Mezzotint after Mr. Whistler's beautiful and famous portrait, we have to thank the artist himself and Messrs. Henry Graves & Co., the fine art publishers, of Pall Mall. The photographs of "Edinburgh Carlyle localities" were specially done by Mr. Thomas Clark for a lecture at the Edinburgh Literary Institute by Mr. James Sims, of Craigmount, and are given by courteous permission of Mr. Alexander Greig, Secretary of the Institute. The portrait of Carlyle and his Niece, with an autograph inscription attached, was kindly lent to us for reproduction by Mr. W. T. Stead.

"WESTMINSTER GAZETTE" OFFICE,
December 4th, 1895.

THE DESK ON WHICH CARLYLE WROTE HIS BOOKS.

CONTENTS

	PAGE
PREFACE	vii
INTRODUCTION: an Address by the Right Hon. Leonard Courtney, M.P.	xv

THE EARLY HOMES OF CARLYLE (By Henry C. Shelley):—

			PAGE
Chapter	I.	Ecclefechan.	3
,,	II.	The House in which Carlyle was born	11
,,	III.	Mainhill	21
,,	IV.	Hoddam Hill	25
,,	V.	Scotsbrig	33

CARLYLE LOCALITIES IN EDINBURGH:—

Chapter	VI.	Carlyle's Student Residences . .	41
,,	VII.	Early Married Life at "Comely Bank."	52
,,	VIII.	A Visit to Carlyle's Niece . . .	57

CARLYLE AT CRAIGENPUTTOCK:—

Chapter	IX.	A General View of Craigenputtock .	71
,,	X.	Life at Craigenputtock .	77

CARLYLE IN LONDON:—

Chapter	XI.	Memorials of Cheyne Row . .	87
,,	XII.	The Story of a Desecrated Shrine	108
,,	XIII.	The Carlyle House as it is . .	115

CONCLUSION: A Visit to Carlyle's Grave .	145

ILLUSTRATIONS

Frontispiece —Mr. Whistler's Portrait of Carlyle.

	PAGE
CARLYLE'S DESK	x
ECCLEFECHAN :—	
The Village Street	4
The Arched House (Carlyle's birthplace) . .	5
The Old School	8
The Old Meeting House	9
THE ROOM IN WHICH CARLYLE WAS BORN . .	15
CARLYLE "CURIOS :"—	
China and Tobacco Jar	12
Lady Ashburton's Tray	13
Carlyle's Hats	14, 17
His Tea Caddy and Coffee-pot	19
His Washing-stand	24
MAINHILL	23

ILLUSTRATIONS

	PAGE
HODDAM HILL:—	
Front View	27
Rear View	28
"Repentance Tower"	31
Hoddam Kirk	32
SCOTSBRIG	35
CARLYLE'S CIGAR-CASE, PIPE, &c.	38
CARLYLE'S FIRST EDINBURGH LODGINGS	47
CARLYLE'S HOUSE IN MORAY STREET, EDINBURGH	50
CARLYLE'S HOUSE, "COMELY BANK"	55
A CARLYLE FAMILY GROUP	59
CARLYLE AND HIS NIECE (Portraits, with autograph inscription)	63
CRAIGENPUTTOCK	73
CARLYLE'S STUDY AT CRAIGENPUTTOCK	79
CARLYLE'S LODGINGS IN WOBURN BUILDINGS	89
NO. 5, CHEYNE ROW, CHELSEA (OUTSIDE)	93
CHELSEA INTERIORS:—	
The Front Door	119
Front Room, ground floor	92
Back Room, ground floor	95
Drawing Room	103
Entrance to Study	104
Sound-proof Study	136
The Kitchen	128
Staircase and Garden	91
A Glimpse of the Garden	101
In the Garden	129

CARLYLE "CURIOS AT CHELSEA:"—

	PAGE
Carlyle's Bookcases	127, 132
Carlyle's Bed	141
Carlyle's Chest of Drawers	114
Mrs. Carlyle's Fire-screen	118
Portrait of Mrs. Carlyle	133
Portrait of Carlyle (about 1860)	137
The Dining Table	121
Carlyle's Sofa	126
Carlyle's Inkstand and Candlestick	125
Carlyle's Study Chair	139
Carlyle's Hat and Hat-box	139
Carlyle's Dinner-plate	131
Drawing-room Chair	139
Brass Fender	139

"A DESECRATED SHRINE:" The Cats at Cheyne Row . 109

CARLYLE ON HIS HORSE "FRITZ" 123

CARLYLE'S GRAVE 146, 147

INTRODUCTION

(*An Address by the Right Hon. Leonard Courtney, M.P.*)

AT the first meeting of the Committee for the purchase of Carlyle's house at Chelsea, an address on the subject was delivered by Mr. Courtney. A gentleman who happened to be present, has been kind enough to send his notes to us, and Mr. Courtney has, further, been at the trouble of revising the report, which we now beg to submit to all admirers of "the Sage of Chelsea." It forms an admirable introduction to the records in the following pages.

"The object of the meeting," said Mr. Courtney, "has been advocated with the utmost force, because with the most perfect sincerity, and I do not think there can be a single person present who has not been touched by the confessions made by Lord Ripon of the influence Carlyle had upon his mind, and by the tribute which has been brought from across the Atlantic of the far-reaching influence of Mr. Carlyle wherever the English language is spoken. I would express for myself, and, I think, many more, the profound indebtedness we are under to that great man who is gone, and the delight we each take in associating ourselves in any way with the means of preserving his memory. I am not one of those who desire indiscriminately to preserve the records of the past. I sometimes look forward to the coming generations with a feeling of pity, when I think how, day by day and almost hour by hour, we are accumulating masses of rubbish under which their lives threaten to be buried. At this very moment, since we have begun to speak, edition after edition of the most ephemeral newspapers have appeared. They will be filed in the British Museum, if not elsewhere, and the scholar of the future will not be able to avoid the duty of submitting them to an examination. Not every house would I preserve. There is some comfort in thinking that there are jerry-builders about and that some habitations will cease. But in Mr. Carlyle I recognise one of the chosen few, one of the elect and select, one to whom it is given—not in every generation, for some pass without such precious possessions

—but one of those to whom it is given from time to time to revive, as it were, the life of humanity, and to bring forth anew the best thoughts, the deepest feelings, the highest aspirations of their fellow-men. Mr. Carlyle himself exhausted words in order to describe the kind of man, the kind of visitor, the angel of mankind, whose work has been realised by men of sensibility, by men of gratitude in every generation. We sometimes speak of a new birth, sometimes of a new creation, sometimes, as Mr. Carlyle would say, of a man or a woman being a child of the Infinite instead of a child of the Finite. All these phrases point to a particular experience through which every man and woman should go when the ordinary life seems to fail, and a new life springs up within them, and they have their feet planted firmly in a large room, and their vision and conception of the world's history undergoes a change. This is what some of us owed to Mr. Carlyle, and if society, literature, the political world of the day, is more or less penetrated with his ideas so that they have not the same quality of newness for us that they had when they were first put before the world, still I believe that the number of readers of Carlyle increases year by year, that the circle of his influence is extended, that new realms are being brought under his sway, that the number of persons who are indebted to him to-day far exceeds that at

b

any previous time. It is because I regard Mr. Carlyle in this way that I desire to associate myself with this movement. And I am certainly not alone. At the instance of the Committee who got up this meeting I wrote and asked our friend Professor Huxley, who is himself on the list of those who promote this enterprise, to come and speak here. He gave two substantial reasons for his inability to attend. He is not young; he is not strong, as he once was; but he wound up with these words:—'I myself deeply regret I cannot say a word of gratitude to the grand old Diogenes-Socrates who dragged me out of the mud of British Philisterei fifty years ago.' Dragged him out of the mud, free from the incumbrances which beset our feet. I do not know whether I shall be thought to have too much of the spirit of Old Mortality when I confess that it is nearly forty years since I made a pedestrian pilgrimage to Craigenputtock. I thought then, and I think still, that the surroundings of Craigenputtock were in complete harmony with 'Sartor Resartus.' I can see now those barren moorlands, with rare stumps of dark fir, and with black sullen tarns among the hills. All corresponded to the fierce troubled spirit out of which that great book came. I was also a pilgrim, but more recently, to Haddington, and I rejoiced there to find the house in which Mrs. Carlyle was born and bred surviving with great dignity and in admirable condition; the drawing-room much as it was when she was the bright young lady who received the young savage from the South. And the house in Cheyne Row, I believe, will be regarded by future generations—for I am quite sure we shall rescue it from the degradation in which it is now—not only as the place where, after that first volume of the 'French Revolution' had been burnt, the husband and wife had that terrible hour together before the whole job was set to over again, and where the other great books of which Lord Ripon has spoken were produced, but will be regarded also as a place where one of the most interesting, pathetic, tragical, and yet fascinating of joint lives was lived. The record has its dark spots, but the dark spots happily passed away before the end. Grateful as one is to Mr. Carlyle, profoundly as I respect him, much as I am his man, I was never his slave any more than Lord Ripon, and though I and Lord Ripon differ in many respects we nevertheless acknowledge what we owe to him. As a husband he showed something too much of the arrogance and isolation of genius. In his want of sensibility to the wife, and in the proud silences of the wife's life, you see something more interesting, something more attractive, than is to be found in any novel. Reality is about it, which, as Carlyle himself would have said, is the first of attributes; reality is about it, reality and pathos, and the unavailing years of regret after her death—all these things are associated with this house in Cheyne-row. The movement is in your hands, and in those of English-speaking people all over the world. Nay, not English-speaking people alone. The German Kaiser has sent his contribution. Wherever manhood is respected, wherever courage and worth are honoured, wherever gratitude is felt towards one of those living spirits who, coming with a coal of fire to touch our lips, bring us again within the world of spirits, there this movement has a claim, and we shall all be proud to assist in making Carlyle's house a temple of resort for future generations."

Part I.

THE EARLY HOMES
OF
CARLYLE.

By HENRY C. SHELLEY.

"*On fine evenings I was wont to carry forth my supper (bread-crumb boiled in milk), and eat it out-of-doors. On the coping of the Orchard-wall, which I could reach by climbing, or still more easily if Father Andrews would set up the pruning ladder, my porridge was placed: there, many a sunset, have I, looking at the distant Western Mountains, consumed, not without relish, my evening meal. Those hues of gold and azure, that hush of World's expectation as Day died, were still a Hebrew Speech for me; nevertheless I was looking at the fair illuminated Letters, and had an eye for their gilding.*"—SARTOR RESARTUS, Book II. Ch. 2, "Idyllic."

CHAPTER I.

ECCLEFECHAN.

A prophet without honour in his own country—Carlyle's birthplace—Where he went to school—The old meeting house.

THERE are no Carlylean hero-worshippers in Ecclefechan, the birthplace of the prophet of that *cultus*. While all the world knows only one Carlyle the natives of the small Annandale town where he was born, a hundred years ago (1795), have a provoking habit of asking pilgrims thither the astounding question, "*Which* Carlyle?" There is a tradition in the district that an old roadman, now dead, happening to be addressed by a party of Carlyle devotees, ran over the names of the various members of the family, and dwelt with special emphasis upon that of Sandy, "who was a grand breeder o' soos." "But there was one called

Thomas, you know," rejoined the leader of the pilgrims. "Ay," retorted the old roadman, "there was Tam; he gaed awa' up to London, but I dinna think he ever did muckle guid."

Futile is the search of the man who goes to Ecclefechan on the look-out for worshippers of Carlyle. And, seemingly, it all arises from the utilitarian way

ECCLEFECHAN : VILLAGE STREET.

the natives have of regarding the most famous member of the Carlyle family. A mild remonstrance addressed to the hotel-keeper on his lack of appreciation in not at least hanging a portrait of the sage in his public room only elicited the grumbling reply, "What did *he* do for the village?" Annandale people are loth to believe any generosity of Thomas Carlyle.

Although built a hundred years ago, the house in which Carlyle was born—called "Arch House," on account of the wide archway running from front to back—shows no signs of decay. It was built by Carlyle's father, an honest mason, who left off rearing houses when the old taste for substantial buildings

ARCH HOUSE.

went out of fashion. "Nothing that he undertook to do," witnessed Carlyle, "but he did it faithfully and like a true man. I shall look on the houses he built with a certain proud interest. They stand firm and sound to the heart all over his little district. No one that comes after him will say, 'Here was the finger of a hollow eye-servant.'"

In front of the Arched House runs a stream. This is the brook which Carlyle refers to in "Sartor," when he says, "The little Kuhbach gushing kindly by— through river after river into the Donaw—(the River Annan), into the Black Sea—(the Solway)." Carlyle's father occupied the top flat on the right hand side, and Carlyle was born in the top room, though his sister used to say that he was not born in that room, but in the small one near the arch. It is on one of the panes of this smaller room that a Member of Parliament cut with a diamond the following lines of poetry :—

> "While Scotland's sons in every clime are found
> Bearing the banner of their country's fame,
> So long will Sartor's laurel be renowned,
> And honest Scots revere his deathless Name."

Changes take place so slowly in Scottish villages that the Ecclefechan of to-day differs but little from the Ecclefechan of Carlyle's boyhood. Buildings once put to one purpose are now put to another, otherwise they remain now as then. And so it happens that the humble building in which Carlyle laid the foundation of his education is still standing, though not now used as a school. One end abuts against the side of the United Presbyterian Church, the other merges into the wall of the kirkyard where Carlyle is buried. Utilised now as a dwelling-house, it is easy to recall the days when it was the *Academia* of the district, so close is its likeness to many a building in other Scottish villages still devoted to educational purposes. Little is remembered of Carlyle's earliest schooldays, and, indeed, it is hardly to be expected that a boy of five would furnish much pabulum for the biographer. A year or two ago there died at Ecclefechan an aged lady who claimed to have attended this school with Carlyle, but her reminiscences did not go beyond that bare fact. The purpose of Carlyle's father in sending him to this school, and afterwards to Annan Academy and Edinburgh University, is well known; he had the desire of every Scottish parent to see his son " wag his pow in a pulpit." Of course the worthy man was wofully disappointed when his son found that such an occupation was impossible for him; but in this, as in so many other unpleasant matters, he consumed his own smoke. "His tolerance for me," said Carlyle, "his trust in me, was great. When I declined going forward into the Church (though his heart was set upon it), he respected my scruples, my volition, and patiently let me have my way." This self-denial becomes more noteworthy in the light of an anecdote related to me in Ecclefechan. It had become known in the village that "Tom Carlyle" was destined for the kirk, and the village gossips were always pressing old James Carlyle with the awkward question, "Why is not Tam coming out for the kirk?" Now, the old man was too proud to own his disappointment to the village gossips, and so one day, when the question was more pointedly put than usual, he rejoined: "Do you think oor Tam is going to stand up and be criticised by a man like Matthie Latimer?"—the said Matthie Latimer being an argumentative theologian of the meeting-house, who was always ready with his remarks upon the pulpit performances gone through there.

The fate which has befallen the school-house has also overtaken the old meeting-house, where, in the

THE OLD SCHOOL.

early years of this century, the young Carlyle heard many an orthodox and long-winded discourse. He never forget those childish experiences, or grew ashamed to confess their influence on his character.

"Poor temple of my childhood," he wrote sixty years after, "to me more sacred at this moment than perhaps the biggest cathedral then extant could have been; rude, rustic, bare—no temple in the world more so—but there were sacred lambencies, tongues of authentic flame from heaven which kindled what was best in one, what has not yet gone out." Strongly attached as old

THE OLD MEETING HOUSE.

James Carlyle was to the Seceders, a trivial incident in the history of the congregation cut him adrift from them for a time. It happened that a new manse was to be built for the minister, and there arose a division of opinion as to the number of rooms it should contain, James Carlyle voting in favour of such a minimum as seemed consistent with a creed which laid more emphasis on the next world than this. His views, however, were not those of the majority, and to mark his disapproval of such a worldly policy as was implied in the erection of too spacious a manse, he left the communion for a time. With characteristic Scottish forethought the old Seceders had several flues placed in their meeting-house at the time of its erection, in anticipation of the day when the congregation should either dwindle away or by the erection of a new building should find it necessary to dispose of the old one. It was the latter contingency that happened, and the old meeting-house, by reason of its flues, was easily transformed into a number of tenements.

CHAPTER II.

THE HOUSE IN WHICH CARLYLE WAS BORN.

Some Carlyle "curios"—Carlyle's hats—An immortal dialogue—Portraits of Carlyle and his wife—From birth-room to kirkyard—The story of a spire.

THE tiny room in which Carlyle was born—it is at the top of the house in the right-hand corner of our view on p. 5—is devoted now to the housing of some interesting mementoes of the infant who drew his first breath there on December 4, 1795. In one corner an unpretentious bookcase holds a copy of the familiar brown-covered "People's Edition" of his writings; a recess near by is filled with bits of old china from the house in Cheyne-row; on the mantelpiece are two turned wooden candlesticks, a gift of John Sterling, sent from Rome; a table in the corner provides a resting place for the philosopher's reading-lamp and tea-caddy; and above a framed letter on the south wall two of his hats are hung. More attention is paid to these hats than to any of the other relics; what higher happiness can the hero-worshipper wish than the being able to say he has had his head inside Carlyle's hat? *Inside* it goes in a quite literal sense. Up to the time of my visit, only

SOME OF THE CHEYNE-ROW CHINA. CARLYLE'S TOBACCO JAR IS IN THE TOP RIGHT-HAND CORNER.

twenty-nine heads had been found to fit that hat; I regret to add that mine did not make the thirtieth. All this applies specially to one hat—a black, wide-brimmed, soft felt; perhaps the identical hat which called forth the immortal dialogue between the passenger and the 'bus driver: "Queer 'at that old fellow 'ad who just got in." "Queer 'at! Ay, he may wear a queer 'at, but what would you give for the 'ed-piece that's a inside of it?" The other hat, just as broad-brimmed, but of straw instead of felt, is none too large for an ordinary cranium—a fact not without its consolatory side. Many tempting offers, most emanating from audacious

MORE CHINA FROM CHEYNE-ROW. THE HAND-PAINTED LUNCH TRAY IN THE CENTRE WAS THE WORK AND GIFT OF LADY ASHBURTON.

Americans, have been made for those hats, and once a bid was couched in this subtle form: "Sell me that hat for £5 and put another old one like it in its place!"

Not far from the hats there is a frame of portraits of Carlyle and his wife, somewhat roughly mounted, but of exceptional interest. Of Carlyle there are six portraits; of his wife, four. One of the portraits of

Carlyle, that bearing the date 1845, ranks among the earliest likenesses of him extant, and has a considerable

CARLYLE'S HAT. INSIDE MEASUREMENT: 23 INCHES.

resemblance to that crayon drawing by Samuel Lawrence of which Carlyle thought so highly that he commended it to Emerson as the most suitable for a frontispiece to

THE ROOM IN WHICH CARLYLE SAID HE WAS BORN.
(From a photograph by Mr. George G. Napier.)

the American edition of his works. While all the
portraits of Carlyle have a strong resemblance to each

CARLYLE'S HAT. INSIDE MEASUREMENT: 24 INCHES.

other and harmonise with most of the portraits that have
been made of him, those of his wife which find a place
in this frame, while consistent with each other, have

little or nothing in common with that graceful and handsome young lady who figures in the second volume of the "Early Letters of Thomas Carlyle." In these portraits Mrs. Carlyle's face recalls that of George Eliot. The brow is high and massive, the eyes deep-sunk and sad, the mouth large and cynical. If Mrs. Carlyle was ever like her Edinburgh portrait of 1826 she must have changed amazingly; if these later portraits represent any physiognomic continuity, the artist of the Edinburgh portrait must have lied amazingly.

In looking at the Arch House from the opposite side of the street, the spire of the United Presbyterian Church is a conspicuous object in the background to the right hand. On the other side of that spire is the Ecclefechan kirkyard, where Thomas Carlyle lies at rest. So do the beginnings and ends of things meet; here the room memorable for its birth, there the kirkyard memorable for its death. That spire brings to memory a Carlyle story told me in the district. Carlyle's father, and the family in general, were adherents of a dissenting congregation known as the Seceders or Associate Congregation, but in 1847 these and other dissenters were merged in the United Presbyterian Church, and henceforward the Carlyle family were reckoned among its members. By-and-by the newly-named congregration addressed themselves to the erection of a new church, and Carlyle's brother James promised a contribution of £50 to the building. Whether James Carlyle made his promise in good faith none can tell, but it is affirmed that the erection of the spire was made the pretext on his part for declining to implement his promise. And so that spire cost £50 more than its contract price. Nor was that all; the

CARLYLE'S TEA-CADDY, TOBACCO-CUTTER, AND COFFEE-POT.

incident terminated by James Carlyle and his family leaving the United Presbyterian Church and becoming members of the Church of Scotland congregation at Middlebie.

Mr. George G. Napier, whose photograph of Carlyle's birth-room we are permitted to reproduce, furnishes the following inventory and further particulars:—" All the furniture came from Cheyne-row except the fender.

The carpet is the old drawing-room one. The hats on the wall I put there; they usually hang on the wall opposite. The one felt; the other straw—his summer one. The clock was his kitchen clock at Chelsea. The lamp was his study lamp. His tobacco-cutter is on the mantelpiece. The portraits about the mantelpiece are those of himself and his mother. The tin box on the table is his tea-caddy. The visitors' book was presented by an American—namely, Mr. Thomas Cook, of Boston. A traveller from Africa once insisted on sleeping on the floor of this room all night, and wrote after his name

"He taught me Truth, Reverence, Earnestness."

CHAPTER III.

MAINHILL.

From mason to farmer—The farm at Mainhill—The Carlyle "family tongue"—Mainhill as it is to-day.

WHEN the mason trade deteriorated to such an extent that honest work went out of fashion, James Carlyle turned to the occupation of farming, "that so he might keep all his family about him." The first farm he took was that known as Mainhill, situated on the great north road, about two miles from Ecclefechan. Here the Carlyles lived from 1815 to 1826. It was not a desirable farm at that time. "A wet, clayey spot," Carlyle describes it, "a place of horrid drudgery;" and in 1825 he writes to his brother Alexander:—
"I hope my father will not think of burdening himself

further with Mainhill and its plashy soil when the lease has expired." Two anecdotes of the Mainhill days, told me in the district, throw a little light upon the domestic history of the family at that period. An old man, Peter Scott by name, who served on the farm at Mainhill as a lad, told my informant that when his day's work was done he took a seat by the kitchen fire and "held my head down for fear ane o' them wad begin on me." All the Carlyles alike, with the possible exception of the mother, were noted, and feared, and hated in Ecclefechan for their caustic tongues, and this incident of the serving lad holding his head down for fear any one of the family would begin on him throws that hatred into sharp relief. The other anecdote concerns the father alone, and is valuable as indicating the origin of Carlyle's apostrophising habit. A gang of saw millers had put up at Mainhill, increasing to an unusual size the company which gathered round the old man when he conducted family worship. His consecutive reading had brought him to that chapter in Genesis where Potiphar's wife figures so infamously with Joseph, and he read it through with his severest enunciation, closing the book with emphatic action as he shouted, "And thou wast a b———!"—a coarse, canine word which seems to have been often on his lips. When his wife was in that unsettled mental state which ultimately prompted her removal from home for a short time, she did a deed that afterwards grieved and appalled herself.

Seeing the old man stooping with a pail for water at the well, she stole forward and pushed him bodily in! Then in a state of mortal terror she rushed into the house, expecting him to well-nigh slay her in an ungovernable passion. To her amazement, however, when she was singing at the pitch of her voice in the

MAINHILL.

pretence of fearing him not, he entered quite calmly and saluted her with, "Well, thou art a merry b —— !"

The wife of the present tenant of Mainhill was kind enough to show me over the house, pointing out the rooms which were in existence when the Carlyles lived there and the additions that have been made since. Mr. J. A. Froude informed me that in my photograph Mainhill is twice the size it used to be, and he added that Carlyle always had unpleasant remembrances of that farm. The chief addition to the house is that two-storeyed wing which occupies the foreground of the picture, other alterations in the rear not affecting the size of the building so much as its convenience.

CARLYLE'S WASHING-STAND AT CHEYNE ROW.

CHAPTER IV.

HODDAM HILL.

Carlyle's removal to Hoddam Hill—"A house in the country, and a horse to ride on"—Carlyle and his landlord—A quarrel and a notice to quit—"Repentance Tower."

AT one period in the early life of Carlyle, when the Church, law, and tutoring had each failed to provide him with an occupation, it occurred to him that he might solve the problem of life by taking a small farm in his native district, where he could study and write in peace, while one of his brothers attended to the necessary practical work of the holding. "A house in the country, and a horse to ride on, I must and will have if it be possible." This was the message which set the Mainhill people on the look-out, and soon they were able to report that in the small farm of Hoddam Hill they had secured the place he needed. Accordingly, Carlyle took possession of Hoddam Hill Farm at the Whitsun Day term, 1825, his mother going with him as housekeeper, and brother Alick as practical farmer. For a wonder, considering the nature of the man, Carlyle was perfectly satisfied with the place. "I have been to see the place," he wrote Miss Welsh, "and I like it well so far as I am interested in it. There is a good house, where I may establish myself in comfortable quarters. The views from it are superb. There are hard, smooth roads to gallop on towards any point of the compass, and ample space to dig and prune under the pure canopy of a wholesome sky. The ancient Tower of Repentance stands on a corner of the farm, a fit memorial for reflecting sinners." This was Carlyle's first impression of the farm, nor did occupancy prove that distance had lent enchantment to the view. "We live here on our hill-top enjoying a degree of solitude that might content the great Zimmermann himself. Few mortals come to visit us, I go to visit none." Long years after he could recall the spot with feelings of unmixed pleasure. "Hoddam Hill," he wrote in his "Reminiscences," "was a neat, compact little farm, rent £100, which my father had leased for me, on which was a prettyish little cottage for dwelling-house, and from the window such a view (fifty miles in radius from beyond Tyndale to beyond St. Bees, Solway Firth, and all the Fells to Ingleborough inclusive) as Britain or the world could hardly have matched." At the present time the Carlyle pilgrim has considerable difficulty in finding Hoddam Hill, the fact of the philosopher's tenancy of that spot having faded from the local

HODDAM HILL: FRONT VIEW.

memory. All my questions were answered with stolid negatives; I must mean Mainhill. Even a man who had lived on the estate all his life was ignorant that Carlyle once rented one of its farms. A twofold explanation offers of this somewhat surprising fact: Carlyle only occupied the farm for a year, and the local name for the house appears to be "The Hill," rather than "Hoddam Hill." If additional proof were wanted of the indifference with which Carlyle is regarded in Annandale, it might be adduced from the deplorable condition of the house in which he lived at Hoddam Hill. The front door has been blocked up, and the building so divided internally that it now

HODDAM HILL: REAR VIEW.

provides shelter for two labourers' families. When I saw the place in the spring of 1893 it was in a condition that would have been disgraceful had it been used as a pig-sty; mud and dirt were plentiful in all directions; heaps of rubbish made walking a gymnastic exercise; fences were broken down and gates lay prostrate; and unwashed and unkempt children looked out from the doorways.

Carlyle may have had some idea of settling down at Hoddam Hill. It was a delightful spot, and admirably adapted to the case of a man who needed perfect quiet and unlimited fresh air. But it was not to be. He himself, however, was, I believe, to blame for starting the sequence of events which led to his removal. It happened in this way. Carlyle rode a great deal at Hoddam, and one day the laird's wife, Mrs. Sharpe, was walking gently down the hill near Repentance Tower, when he passed her on his horse. As soon as he got in front of her, he put his horse to the gallop with such violence that the lady was soundly besplashed with mud from head to foot. It was after this ungallant incident, as I was informed, that the laird, General Sharpe, called at Hoddam Hill, and Carlyle went to him at the door, declining to ask him in. They had a battle royal of words, and the General brought matters to a crisis by asking with a sneer, " *You*, what do YOU know about farming?" After this thunder came the Carlylean lightning. "One thing I can do," he shouted, " I can pay the rent. That's all you have to do with the land, and I'll feed laverocks on it if I like." Then he slammed the door in the irate General's face. Carlyle had often wished for a door of his own, which he might " slam in the face of all nauseous intrusions," and he had got it now, and used it! But he was not to have it for long. No laird would endure such treatment from a tenant; at any rate, General Sharpe was not the man to endure it. And so Carlyle had to quit Hoddam Hill, and look about for a new home.

During his year at Hoddam Hill, a year which abode as "a russet-coated idyll" in his memory because of the visit Miss Welsh paid him there, Carlyle had two objects in his landscape in which he took a deep interest, and they are of interest to us because his eyes rested upon them so often, and also because there are so many allusions to them in his letters. Chief of these was Repentance Tower, a solemn-looking building which stood near the house, but a little higher up on the hill. It is surrounded by a graveyard, and hangs there so spectral amid its memorials of the dead that it might furnish food for thought to sinners of a less reflecting turn of mind than Carlyle. The cause of its erection and the origin of its name are thus related. A certain Lord Herries—identified as the champion of Mary Queen of Scots—was famous among those who, three or four centuries ago, made forays into the English border. On one occasion, when returning with many prisoners, he was overtaken by a storm while crossing the Solway, and in order to lighten his boat, cut all their throats and cast them into the sea. Some time after, feeling great qualms of conscience, he built this sturdy tower, carving over the door the figures of a dove and serpent, emblems of remorse and grace, with the word "Repentance" between them. The other prominent object in Carlyle's landscape was Hoddam

REPENTANCE TOWER.

Kirk, a low-lying and rather picturesque little building with a curious little tower. In that tower hung the bell to which he makes a pathetic allusion in his reminiscences of life at Hoddam Hill. "My thoughts were very peaceable, full of pity and humanity—as they had never been before. Nowhere can I recollect of myself such pious musings, communings silent and spontaneous with fact and nature, as in those poor Annandale localities. The sound of the kirk-bell once

HODDAM KIRK.

or twice on Sunday mornings (from Hoddam Kirk, about a mile on the plains below me) was strangely touching, like the departing voice of eighteen hundred years."

CHAPTER V.

SCOTSBRIG.

THE abrupt termination of Carlyle's tenancy of Hoddam Hill coincided with the expiry of his father's lease of Mainhill, and there had to be a double flitting. Once more there was diligent searching through the countryside for a desirable farm, rewarded at length by the discovery of Scotsbrig,* which was to remain the family home for the rest of Carlyle's life. Scotsbrig is so closely interwoven with the history of his books that his word-pictures of the place, both in anticipation and realisation, deserve to be added to those provided by the camera. In anticipation, he wrote to his brother

* "The farm," says Mr. Napier, "is very nicely situated above a little brook which runs through a sort of glen. Over this brook was once a sort of natural bridge—hence the name God's-brig, corrupted into Scotsbrig."

John:—" By dint of unbounded higgling, and the most consummate diplomacy, the point was achieved to complete satisfaction of the two husbandmen [Carlyle's father and Alick]; and Scotsbrig, free of various 'clags and claims,' which they had argued away, obtained for a rent of £190 (cheap, as they reckon it), in the face of many competitors. . . . The people also are to repair the house effectually; to floor it anew, put *bun*-doors on it, new windows, and so forth; and it seems it is an excellent *shell* of a house already. . . . Our mother declares that there is 'plenty of both *prats* and water;' others think 'the farm is the best in Middlebie parish*in*'; our father seems to have renewed his youth, even as the eagle's age." Two months later Carlyle wrote to John again, this time in realisation:—"We are all got over with whole bones to this new country; and every soul of us, our mother to begin with, much in love with it. The house is in bad order; but we hope to have it soon repaired, and for farming purposes it is an excellent 'shell of a house.' Then we have a *linn* with crags and bushes and a 'fairy knowe,' though no fairies that I have seen yet; and, cries our mother, abundance of grand thready peats, and water from the brook, and no reek, and no Honour (*i.e.*, General Sharpe) to pester us! To say nothing, cries our father, of the eighteen *yeacre* of the best barley in the county; and bog-hay, adds Alick, to fatten scores of young

SCOTSBRIG. (*From a photograph by Mr. George G. Napier.*)

beasts! In fact, making all allowance for new fangledness, it is a *much* better place, so far as I can judge, than any our people have yet been in; and among a far better and kindlier sort of people."

Such was Scotsbrig in 1826, and such it remains to the present day. Here Carlyle's father and mother lived for the remainder of their days, and here his brother James kept the old home together until within a few years of his own death. Here, too, Carlyle spent the most of his holidays; for even after he became famous, and could have passed those holidays in the homes of the greatest of the land, he generally elected to spend his days of rest among his own kindred in this unpretentious but peaceful home. It is well known that Carlyle suffered severely in writing his books. Most authors do. No book that is worth writing is written without a great expenditure of nervous and mental force. At any rate it was so with Carlyle. When he had finished a book he felt completely prostrate, and to recover strength and spirit again he generally fled to Scotsbrig. What Virgil did for Dante at the foot of Purgatory, Scotsbrig did for Carlyle when he emerged from the Inferno into which his books plunged him.

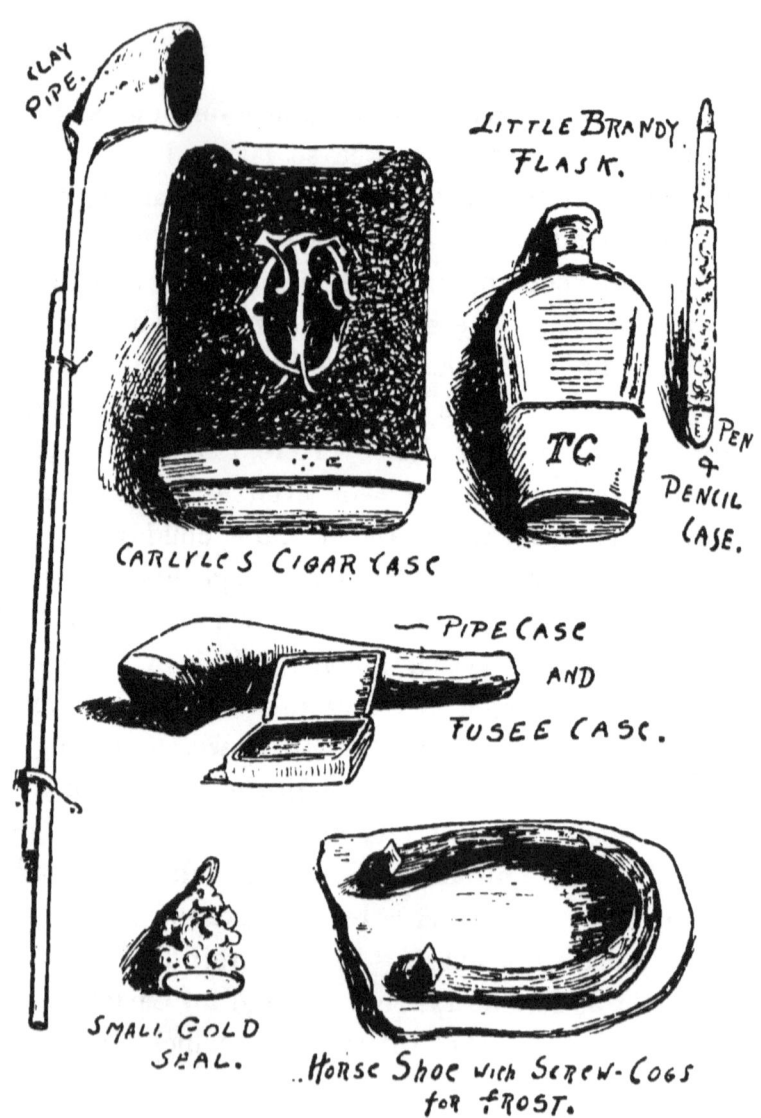

SOME CARLYLE RELICS.

Part II.

CARLYLE LOCALITIES

in

EDINBURGH.

"'There is a country accent,' says La Rochefoucault, 'not in speech only, but in thought, conduct, character and manner of existing, which never forsakes a man'... A country whence the entire people is, or even once has been, laid hold of, filled to the heart with an infinite religious idea, has 'made a step from which it cannot retrograde.' Thought, conscience, the sense that man is denizen of a Universe, creature of an Eternity, has penetrated to the remotest cottage, to the simplest heart. Beautiful and awful, the feeling of a Heavenly Behest, of Duty God-commanded, over-canopies all life."—ESSAY ON SIR WALTER SCOTT (Miscellanies, vol. vi.).

CHAPTER VI.

CARLYLE'S STUDENT RESIDENCES.

Carlyle as an Edinburgh man—His student lodgings—Life at the Universities—Carlyle's inscription on a window pane.

AT the first conference in Edinburgh for the celebration of the hundredth birthday of Thomas Carlyle, on 4th December, 1895, Emritus-Professor Masson alluded to the purchase of Carlyle's house in Cheyne Row, and how people from all parts of the world were going to see the house in which he lived and worked. There ought, he thought, to be commemoration of Carlyle also in Scotland, and particularly in Edinburgh. The earlier part of Carlyle's life, and a very critical time of his life, intellectually, was spent in Edinburgh; he was an Edinburgh man for a part of his life; he was educated at Edinburgh University; he was a citizen of

Edinburgh; the houses in which he lived successively were still shown. In his old age, when laden with honour, he came back to Edinburgh, to receive, what Professor Masson believed Carlyle regarded as the crowning honour of his life, the Lord Rectorship of the University. Carlyle afterwards showed his affection for Edinburgh University by bequeathing to it the estate of Craigenputtock.

The localities directly associated with the Carlyles are his various student lodgings, both in the old and the new town, and No. 21, Comely Bank, in the northern or Stockbridge suburb of Edinburgh, and the scene of his early married life for eighteen months. According to Alison Hay Dunlop, Carlyle previously rented the first flat of the corner tenement of Carlton Street and St. Bernard's Crescent, Mr. Irving, of the Advocate's Library, acting for the proprietor, who was then abroad. He entered into possession, but having conceived, not without reason, some dislike to a neighbouring tenant of questionable reputation, he overwhelmed Mr. Irving with a whirlwind of speech, and cancelled the agreement.

Thomas Carlyle came up from Ecclefechan, Dumfriesshire, to attend Edinburgh University for the November term in 1809, when scarcely fourteen years of age. His companion was Tom Smail, two or three years older than himself: they walked all the way, and took three days to do the journey of 60 miles, which can now be accomplished by Caledonian Railway in a couple of hours. According to the recollections jotted down at Mentone in January, 1867, he had a view of the "Outer House" in Parliament Square, on that very evening of his arrival on November 9th. Everything must have been full of wonder to him as he had never been out of Dumfries-shire before. On the way thither he pictures Tom Smail (afterwards a Burgher minister in Galloway) stalking on in front, whistling an Irish tune, the "Belfast Shoemaker," "most melancholy to poor me, given up to my bits of reflections in the silence of the moors and hills." Carlyle and his companion had secured a clean-looking, and cheap lodging, in a poorer part of the south side of the town off Nicholson Street, called Simon Square. Carlyle's signature may be seen still in the Matriculation Album of the University. It is a clear, firm boyish hand, the sixth signature in the letter C, the previous signature being that of a Dumfries boy, named Irvin Carlyle, who turns up in juxtaposition more than once again. According to Masson the quadrangle was not as it now appears in the University, but a "chaotic jumble of inconvenient old class-rooms," with only parts of the present buildings furnished and occupied. Carlyle attended Professor Alexander Christian for Latin, during his first session, and Professor George Dunbar for Greek. We do not know what kind of scholar he was at this date, but it is certain he had paid his guinea in December entitling him to the use of books in the University Library; and in January, 1810, the Library record shows that he had borrowed and doubtless read "Robertson's History of Scotland, Vol. II;" "Cook's Voyages;" "Byron's Narrative on the Coast of Patagonia;" the first volume of "Gibbon" (afterwards completed at Kirkcaldy); two volumes of "Shakespeare;" a volume of the "Arabian Nights;" "Congreve's Works;" then another volume of the "Arabian Nights;" two volumes of "Hume's England;" "Gil Blas;" a third volume of "Shakespeare," and a volume of the "Spectator." Carlyle was home at Ecclefechan in April, 1810, and was met by his father, on the road, " with a red plaid about him." In his second session 1810–11 he attended the first mathematical class under Professor John Leslie, and the logic class under Professor David Ritchie. His reading from the University Library between December, 1810, and March, 1811, included, were "Voyages and Travels," Fielding, Smollett, Reid's "Inquiry into the Human Mind," "Scotland Described," "Locke's Essays," "Don Quixote," &c. In his third session he attended the second Greek class, the second mathematical, and the moral philosophy under Dr. Thomas Brown; in his last and fourth session when he became a virtual M.A., he was under Leslie again and Playfair for moral philosophy. "Carlyle" says Masson, "when he left our University in 1813, a virtual M.A., aged seventeen years and four months, was already potentially the very Carlyle we now revere, in consequence of his subsequent life, as one of the greatest and noblest spirits of his generation. Not yet at his full stature, and of thin, lean rather gaunt frame, he was a youth of as great faculty, as noble a promise, as Scotland had produced since her Burns, born in 1753, and her Scott, born in 1771." Even then he had a settled literary ambition, but it is hardly the place here to see how this was worked out. We must say something of his Edinburgh homes.

There is a mine of interesting material regarding the formative period of Carlyle's life, and also his Edinburgh life, in the four volumes of *Early Letters*, edited by Professor Norton. When student and teacher he seems to have flitted from lodging to lodging, both in the old town and new town of Edinburgh, with many a grumble in the process, and we are not sure that we have detected all his residences as the heading of his letters is frequently "Edinburgh" only. In November to January, 1818–19, he seems to have lived with a certain Mrs. Davies, in South Richmond Street, and many are the complaints of his landlady's sluttish ways, as also of dirt and vermin. His bill of 15*s*. 2*d*.

for one week, he says, is too much for the slender accommodation and his paltry ill-cooked morsel. "There is a schoolmaster above, thrown in, who has a vocal evening each week, and many noisy brats." By February, 1819, he is away from this lodging and dates from Mrs. Scott's, 15, Carnegie Street, and is careful to tell his mother that he is as anxious as she can possibly be about his own health, walking out before breakfast, and having a stroll in the suburbs after his German lessons, at 11 A.M. In November he is residing with the wife of a tailor named Thomson, paying 6s. a week for his room, fire included. He cannot have remained long here, as he dates in December, from Duff's lodgings, 35, Bristo Street. All these places are in the poorer portion of the old town, and in the south side. In November, 1821, he has taken a jump to the new town, and dates from 9, Jamaica Street. Next month (19th Dec.) he is in Cuisine's lodgings, 5, College Street, a street in the old town, close by, and running parallel to the University. His address during 1822, and part of 1823, was most frequently 3, Moray Street (now Spey Street), off Leith Walk; and 1, Moray Street after the Buller tutorship, in February, 1824. In January, 1826, we find an address from 21, Salisbury Street, a steep street running into the Queen's Park, under the shadow of Salisbury Crags, Arthur's Seat.

Like Burns at Ellisland, and elsewhere, Carlyle left

CARLYLE'S FIRST EDINBURGH LODGING.

a record of his presence and moods sometimes on the window panes. In his lodging at 3, Moray Street, there was a pane of glass, coveted by Mr. Froude for some public institution, and which would be invaluable for the Carlyle Museum, Chelsea, in which he had inscribed the verse of a ballad:

> " O little did my mother think,
> The day she cradled me,
> The lands that I should travel in,
> The death I was to die."

It appears that on the sale of the house, some years ago, this scratched pane of glass was sold to Mr. A. Brown, bookseller, Bristo Place, in September, 1888. This Moray Street residence is one of the most interesting of his Edinburgh abodes, for after abandoning the Church, law, and school-mastering, in turn, he took up his literary work in earnest here, writing articles for Brewster's "Edinburgh Encyclopædia," translating Legendre's "Geometry," and beginning his German translations. It was in this neighbourhood, too, consciously while on Leith Walk, that Carlyle began to take a brighter, braver outlook on life. This was in June, 1821, and is described in "Sartor Resartus" under the guise of Teufelsdröckh traversing Rue St. Thomas de l'Enfer (Leith Walk). From this hour he dates his spark of new birth, "perhaps I directly thereupon began to be a man."

S. T. Coleridge, in a letter to Southey in 1803, after a visit to Edinburgh, exclaimed, "What a wonderful city Edinburgh is! What alternation of height and depth." He enjoyed a sunset from Arthur's Seat immensely. Scott, in his "Heart of Midlothian," has

CARLYLE'S HOUSE, 1, MORAY STREET (NOW SPEY STREET), LEITH WALK.

eulogised Salisbury Crags as the best place from which to witness a sunset; and there Campbell composed some of his finest poetry. This is what Carlyle makes of it, in a letter to his brother in March, 1821; he was hungering for the work of his life, living hazily ahead, and he felt with all its drawbacks Edinburgh was the place for him. 'I am considerably clearer than I was, and I should have been still more so had not this afternoon been wet, and so prevented me from breathing the air of Arthur's Seat, a mountain close beside us, where the atmosphere is pure as a diamond, and the prospect grander than any you ever saw. The blue majestic everlasting ocean, with the Fife hills swelling gradually into the Grampians behind; rough crags and rude precipices at our feet (where not a hillock rears its head unsung), with Edinburgh at their base clustering proudly over her rugged foundations, and covering with a vapoury mantle the jagged black venerable masses of stonework that stretch far and wide, and show like a city of Fairyland. . . . . I saw it all last evening when the sun was going down, and the moon's fine crescent, like a pretty silver creature as it is, was riding quietly above me."

CHAPTER VII.

EARLY MARRIED LIFE AT COMELY BANK.

Literary and artistic associations—Married life—Visits from Jeffrey.

THE late Sir James T. Simpson was never tired of eulogising the healthy nature of the Stockbridge district, in which lies 21, Comely Bank, the residence for eighteen months of Thomas Carlyle after his marriage, 1826–28. Simpson's theory was that the prevailing west and north winds cleared the district of smoke. Now, that the Water of Leith purification scheme is completed, this may be even more the case. Neither is the district without its literary associations. Sir Henry Raeburn and David Roberts were both born there. If we approach Comely Bank from the high road, over one of Telford's last bridges, the Dean, spanning the Water of Leith, a noble prospect broadens to the north-west towards the Firth of Forth, Fife, and westwards the finely wooded Corstorphine Hill, in a nook of which, at Craigbrook, stands the last residence of Lord Jeffrey. Dr. John Brown relates how when walking along here one Sunday evening with Thackeray, a building crane on Corstorphine Hill, the image of a cross, drew from the novelist the single expression, "Calvary." The entrance to the Dean Cemetery is opposite Comely Bank, and here, amongst others of the mighty dead, are buried Lords Jeffrey and Cockburn, Professors John Wilson and Aytoun, and Alexander Russel, of the *Scotsman*. Professor Wilson lived for many a day, and wrote many "Blackwood" articles in Ann Street, near by. Stewart's Hospital, this palatial building to the left, is now one of the Merchants' Company's Schools. That fine building at Comely Bank is Fettes College, an endowed school, and that other beyond is St. Cuthbert's Poor-house. Descending this way to the right from the Queensferry Road, we pass what was in Carlyle's day the fields and steading of the Dean Farm. The town has crept westwards a good deal since then. But 21, Comely Bank, now occupied by Mr. Rhind, sculptor, is still in the country, and there are still no houses opposite. Comely Bank is built of white, hard Craigleith stone, from the quarry close by. The cable cars start every few minutes for the city end of Comely Bank to climb one of the steepest inclines in the New Town, towards Princes Street.

In May, 1826, Carlyle recorded, "House in Comely Bank suitable as possible has been chosen; was being furnished from Haddington, beautifully, perfectly, and even richly, by Mrs. Welsh's great skill in such matters, aided by her daughter's, which was also great, and by the frank, *wordless* generosity of both, which surely was very great." For immediate expenses of living Carlyle had £200; his health and prospects improved during the eighteen months here. He wrote two articles on Jean Paul and on German literature: a paper on Werner, on Goethe's "Helena," and one on Goethe himself, which is reprinted in the "Miscellanies." A novel "Wotton Reinfred" was begun here, which Froude says was burned: but this seems surely not the case, for it seems that this is the same book which appeared in the "New Review" not so long ago. Plenty of visitors called, Jeffrey found them here, and became a true friend to Carlyle and his wife. Jane Carlyle wrote to her mother-in-law, "I should be very stupid or very thankless if I did not congratulate myself, every hour of the day, on the lot which it has pleased Providence to assign me: my husband is so kind! so, in all respects after my own heart. I was sick one day, and he nursed me as well as my own mother could have done." The weekly household expenditure was reckoned at two pounds, which Carlyle believed he could save for them. This seems to have been a happy period in the lives of both. "Directly

CARLYLE'S HOUSE, COMELY BANK.

after breakfast," wrote Carlyle, " the good wife and the doctor (his brother, John Carlyle, now staying with them) retire upstairs to the drawing room, a little place all fitted up like a lady's work-box, where a spunk of fire is lit for the forenoon ; and I, meanwhile, sit scribbling and meditating and wrestling with the powers of dullness till one or two o'clock, when I sally forth into the city or towards the seashore, taking care only to be home for the important purpose of consuming my mutton chop at four. After dinner we all read learned languages till coffee (which we now often take at night instead of tea), and so on till bed-time; only that Jane often sews; and the doctor goes up to the celestial globe, studying the fixed stars through an up-shoved window." Wednesday night was their evening at home, and Brewster, De Quincey, Sir William Hamilton, and Professor Wilson, were amongst the callers. By Jane's request he was to read a sermon and a chapter with commentary, at least every Sabbath Day, and sittings were even taken, although we have no record of how often they were occupied, in the Established Church of St. George's, at the west end. A memorable letter arrived from Goethe, "extremely graceful, affectionate, and patriarchal." Old Mrs. Carlyle paid them a visit and was dragged round the sights of the city, and was not denied "her smoke" in the evening. All this came to an end in May, 1827, when the home was broken up and the household gods were packed to the moorland estate of Craigenputtock. Jeffrey, with his usual kindness, kept the Carlyles for a week in Moray Place, until their furniture should have arrived and matters smoothed for them.

CHAPTER VIII.

A VISIT TO CARLYLE'S NIECE.

Carlyle's niece and companion—Carlyle "curios"—A visit to her house.

MARY CARLYLE AITKEN died at 30, Newbattle Terrace, Edinburgh, on May 30, 1895, of pneumonia, following influenza. She was the daughter of Jean Carlyle, youngest sister of Thomas Carlyle, and was born in Dumfries in 1848. She came into notice as the housekeeper, companion, and amanuensis of her uncle in his later life. She was married in September, 1879, to one of her Canadian cousins, Mr. Alexander Carlyle, B.A., of the Bield, Ontario. The marriage was solemnized by the Rev. James A. Campbell, parish minister of Traquair. Her uncle was able to be present, and entered into conversation with the minister, expressing his gratitude to Almighty God for being spared so long, and speaking also of the work of John Knox. There are two boys of this marriage.

Under her uncle's will she received the manuscript and letters which formed the basis of the Jane Welsh Carlyle "Letters and Memorials," "to whom also, dear little soul, I bequeath £500 for the loving care and unwearied patience and helpfulness she has shown to me in these last solitary and infirm years. To her also I give at her choice whatever memorials of my dear departed one she has seen me silently preserving here, especially the table in the drawing-room, at which I now write, and the little child's chair (in the china closet), which latter to my eyes has always a brightness as of morning, and a sadness as of death and eternity when I look on it, and which, with the other dear article, I have the weak wish to preserve yet awhile when I am gone." On the death of her uncle, John Aitken Carlyle, she was to get all the belongings at Cheyne Row, with few exceptions; but John Carlyle pre-deceased his eminent brother by several years.

Her home at 30, Newbattle Terrace, Edinburgh, was stored with many precious relics of the Carlyle household; and an account of Carlyle localities in Edinburgh would therefore hardly be complete without some reference to the home of Mrs. Alexander Carlyle. A

Provost Swan.   John Carlyle.   Thomas Carlyle.
                                Mary Carlyle Aitken.

TAKEN AT KIRKCALDY.

Photo. by Patrick, 52, Comiston Road, Edinburgh.

representative of the "Westminster Gazette," who paid a visit in 1894 to Mrs. Carlyle, wrote the following account of what he saw.

Mrs. Alexander Carlyle (Mary Carlyle Aitken) had much to do, it should be stated, in stocking the birth-place of Carlyle at Ecclefechan with relics, and took much interest in the purchase of the house at Cheyne Row for a Carlyle Museum. Unfortunately she did not live to see the completion of the scheme, but her husband, Mr. Alexander Carlyle, is doing his utmost to carry out her wishes in the matter.

The proposal to buy the Carlyle house in Cheyne Row was the occasion of the visit described in the following pages:—

Few people, as it appears to me, can be better entitled to express an authoritative opinion as to the desirability of preserving the house at Chelsea in which Carlyle and his gifted wife lived so long, in which he worked, and in which he died, than the niece who was, as he expressed it to Emerson, "useful here as a cheerful rushlight in this now sombre element . . . in which she bears me company." Accordingly I used the kindness of a friend to procure an introduction to Mrs. Alexander Carlyle, and paid a long and delightful visit to her home in Edinburgh.

The house in which she has taken up her temporary abode seemed to me far more redolent of Carlyle than the dismantled dwelling at Cheyne Row can at present possibly be. The furniture which fills it—simple without lack of comfort, and handsome without ostentation—is the same that began its service before the birth of little Jane in Dr. Welsh's home at Haddington, that served Carlyle and his wife from the time of their marriage onwards until the end of their days, successively at Comely Bank in Edinburgh, at lonely Craigenputtock, and at Chelsea, and is still carefully preserved as a precious heirloom. The walls are covered with the portraits of the Carlyle family and their friends. There are Carlyle himself and his wife in more than one rendering; there is, in a place of honour, the fine life-size portrait of Carlyle's mother in her "mutch" that used to hang over the mantelshelf at Cheyne Row; portraits of John Sterling and his mother, of Walter Savage Landor and David Hume, endless prints and other portraits of Frederick the Great and his whole generation, of Cromwell and Shakespeare, Milton and Dante, and many another of Carlyle's heroes. Nor may I forget to mention a beautiful drawing of the dining-room at Cheyne Row by Mrs. Allingham. The books, too, would demand an interview to themselves to do them justice—such books they are! One case in particular is rich with materials for the historian of literature, and with suggestion for the imaginative student. In it are placed almost

entirely the books with inscriptions, and I spent a half-hour, whose fascination only the confirmed bookman can guess, in examining some of its treasures under the guidance of Mrs. Carlyle. There is, for instance, an old quarto Bible containing a childish scrawl that may be safely presumed to be the very earliest autograph of Thomas Carlyle now in existence. A daintily bound set of the complete works in early editions contained in almost every volume some tender and touching dedication to his wife, which, with many another inscription, I would gladly have copied. But although I saw the names of Browning, Tennyson, Ruskin, Leigh Hunt, Thackeray, Emerson, and George Eliot, not to speak of Gœthe, written on rare books, I had to consent with regret to leave them in obscurity. For though Mrs. Carlyle was generous in showing her treasures, she was miserly in her determination that no further description of them should at present go abroad. She consented to be "interviewed," but only on the scheme for purchasing the house in Cheyne Row; "for that," she said, "is a matter which both I and my husband are greatly interested in, and desire to further:"—

"Really, being interviewed isn't so very formidable," I protested. "It's a little like amateur photography, you know—you press a button and I do the rest."— "Alas," she replied, "I know well enough what it's like, and that sometimes the little brown pictures are

E

by no means to one's mind after the button has been pressed. However, if you will ask questions, I will answer them."

"Very well," I said. "In the first place, what do you think generally of the proposed plan for buying the Cheyne Row house, and keeping it as a memorial of Mr. Carlyle?"—"I think it will be delightful, if it can be carried out. I am sure that a great many people would like to look over the house, and it is disgusting to think of it in its present condition."

"You think there would be a good many visitors, if the scheme were carried out?"—"Undoubtedly I think there would. For even to the house at Ecclefechan in which my uncle was born, which is comparatively very inaccessible, there must have been more than 600 visitors in the course of the present year, and I fancy it would be far less interesting to most people than Cheyne Row."

"Are there many portraits of Mr. Carlyle in existence?" I asked.—"Oh, a good many. There are, for instance, the portraits by Lawrence, by Maclise, by Watts, by Millais (I do not know what has become of it), and by Whistler, not to mention many of less note. Then there are early daguerreotypes and photographs also, and the bust by Woolner, and, in addition to the big statue, several things by Boehm. I feel sure that if the house were secured, there would be no difficulty in making it interesting and attractive to visitors. As to that, I am not one of those who think that my uncle will soon be forgotten, or that the books he wrote will soon cease to interest people in all that belonged to him."

Before I left, Mrs. Carlyle took me to see the autographs. These were in another room, where we disturbed from "lessons" a couple of sturdy boys whose rosy cheeks promise long endurance to the Carlyle race in the land. There, framed and hanging behind the door, were the signatures of almost "everybody as was anybody" in the world of letters in 1875, attached to the address of congratulation on the sage's eightieth birthday. "Only twenty years ago!" said Mrs. Carlyle to me, meditatively. "Yet you see how many of them are dead. Tennyson and Browning, Owen and Darwin, Sir Henry Maine and J. R. Green, are all gone." And so I left the house, musing partly on the uncertainty of life, but rather with a wistful eye upon the eternity of well-earned fame.

Part III.

CARLYLE

AT

CRAIGENPUTTOCK.

"*What is Hope?*—*a smiling rainbow*
Children follow through the wet;
'Tis not here, still yonder, yonder!
Never urchin found it yet.

What is Life?—a thawing ice-board
On a sea with sunny shore.
Gay we sail—it melts beneath us!
We are sunk, and seen no more.

What is Man?—a foolish baby;
Vainly strives, and fights and frets;
Demanding all—deserving nothing!
One small grave is what he gets."

Verses by Carlyle, written at Craigenputtock.

CHAPTER IX.

A GENERAL VIEW OF CRAIGENPUTTOCK.

A visit to Craigenputtock—The silence of the moors—Carlyle at Burns's cottage.

CRAIGENPUTTOCK is the lonely farm-house on the borders of Galloway, and in the south-west of Dumfries-shire, where Thomas Carlyle spent seven of the earlier years of his married life (1828-34). This farm, of 1,000 acres or so, he left, as already mentioned, to Edinburgh University. James Carlyle, a nephew, was in occupation, before the death of his uncle in 1881, and now the place is farmed by his widow. There are six young Carlyles at least, and it was a grand-niece, with prominent dark eyes and dark hair, who, in the absence of her mother, showed us over the house.

When Ralph Waldo Emerson came, armed with a letter of introduction, to visit Carlyle, in August, 1833, he landed in the coach at Dumfries from Glasgow. He had to hire for the remaining sixteen miles, and " found the house among desolate heathery moors, where the lonely scholar nourished his mighty heart." Auldgirth Station, on the Glasgow and South Western Railway, is within eight miles of this lonely farm. We took a more interesting but circuitous route to reach the place. One fine Saturday morning, we started from our country quarters just where the brawling Euterkin joins the Nith, and made our way past Drumlanrig, a seat of the Duke of Buccleuch, passed through the villages of Penpont and Moniaive, and following the moorland road to Dalry in Galloway for a few miles, struck southward over an even wilder and lonelier road amongst the hills, with Loch Urr to the left and making a great circuit, reached Craigenputtock. The return journey was by Dunscore Valley and Penpont. Our cycle flew down hill over the shin-stone strewed road. But, as might be expected, the rough cross moorland roads round Craigenputtock are unridable. It is worth remembering in passing Penpont that an enthusiastic Dumfriesian has proved to a demonstration that Macmillan, a blacksmith there, was the pioneer maker of the safety cycle. The story of his doings is as entertaining as a romance. But we leave that to

CRAIGENPUTTOCK. (*From a photograph by Mr. George G. Napier.*)

Mr. Johnstone, of Glasgow. Moniaive lies in fine pastoral scenery in the valley of the Cairn. Maxwelltown, three miles below, is the scene of the song of "Annie Laurie" beginning—

> "Maxwelltown's braes are bonnie."

Moniaive, a village of low slated houses, was the birthplace of James Renwick, the last Scottish martyr. There is a very plain monument to him in the outskirts of the village.

As we skirted lonely Loch Urr with its remains of an ancient Caledonian town, the silence on the moor was almost oppressive. Could we have crossed the moor direct, two miles would have brought us to Craigenputtock. By road it was four miles at least. But we did not regret this, for we crossed Drumwhinn Bridge over the Orr, built in 1832, and celebrated by Carlyle in a poem in Leigh Hunt's journal. It is quite characteristic of the man who said that the builder of a good bridge was greater than the writer of a book.

> Meek autumn midnight glancing,
>   The stars above hold sway,
> I bend, in muse advancing
>   To lonesome Orr my way.
>
> Its rush in drowsy even
>   Can make the waste less dead;
> Short pause beneath void heaven,
>   Then back again to bed.

* * * * * *

> The shinstone bridge is builded,
>   Will hang a hundred year;
> When bridge to time has yielded,
>   The brook will still be here.
>
> Farewell, poor moorland river,
>   We parted and we met;
> Thy journeyings are for ever,
>   Mine are not ended yet.

His journeyings ended about half a century later, for this was written in 1832. This square, two-storey farm-house is protected by a belt of trees, oak, plane, and a few firs. The farmer's wife over at Ellisland remembers a visit made by Carlyle, along with his niece (Mary Carlyle Aitken), about three years before his death. The sage as he looked at the tiny farm-house where Burns wrote "Tam O'Shanter," and "To Mary in Heaven," remarked, "No, there are no relics of Burns here, but perhaps his hand touched this wall."

CHAPTER X.

LIFE AT CRAIGENPUTTOCK.

Carlyle memorials—Some interesting books—Mrs. Carlyle on her banishment.

THERE is the impression of both the head, heart and hand of Thomas Carlyle and Jane Welsh Carlyle about Craigenputtock. The house was built by them and the famous essay on Burns and "Sartor" took shape in this solitude, ere Carlyle exchanged these moorland solitudes for the roar of London. In this pleasant parlour are the Carlyle portrait of 1863; the Hyde Park equestrian photograph, with F. Chapman, the publisher, near the horse's head; the morning room at Chelsea; two excellent portraits of Jane Welsh Carlyle. Here also are portraits of Cromwell (1648), of Frederick the Great's Grandfather in his 27th and 63rd year. Two portraits in the dining-room of Dr. John Carlyle, translator of Dante, remind one strongly of Thackeray. But this snug little room, with its window looking into the back regions of the farm-house is the most interesting place at Craigenputtock. Here, round a good fire, Carlyle defied the elements and the loneliness; "buried himself in his books, and the Devil might pipe to his own," and here he did some of the best and greatest literary work done in the early part of the century. In the book-case here are first editions of most of Carlyle's books. Here is the copy of the "French Revolution" in full calf, which Carlyle sent with a kind inscription to his mother. Another inscription at her death gifted it to his nephew, James Carlyle, of Craigenputtock. It was a kindly touch on the part of Carlyle to insert a little fly-leaf, with a translation, in his own hand, of the motto from Goethe, for the benefit of his mother. Then there is Theobald's "Shakespeare" in eight volumes, also a gift to nephew James for the dark nights at Craigenputtock. There is the usual visitors' book (we found one even at Ellisland, with the names of many Americans inscribed), and some contemporary literature, including "Great Thinkers and Workers" with Carlyle's head emblazoned on the cover.

Craigenputtock (the craig or shinstone hill of the

CARLYLE'S STUDY AT CRAIGENPUTTOCK. (*From a Photograph by Mr. George G. Napier.*)

"puttocks" or small hawks) had been in the Welsh family for many generations. Through Jane Baillie Welsh, only daughter of Dr. Welsh of Haddington, the small estate came to Carlyle, and by him was left to Edinburgh University. Mrs. Welsh had her life-rent of it. As practical man on the spot Alexander Carlyle with his sister went into occupation in 1827. Thomas Carlyle and his wife came thither from Edinburgh in June, 1828, when Jane Carlyle watched the joiners and plumbers, the fowls hatching in the wood, and was up most of the night once, making experiments with the kitchen oven in bread-making, in order to produce bread that would suit Carlyle's stomach. We thought of all this, as we surveyed the kitchen fire-place. Lord Jeffrey, who was patronising Carlyle at this time, broke the quiet of Craigenputtock twice, by a visit. He thought the sage a fool of the first water to settle here. Carlyle noted that he had finished Burns at this "Devil's Den," September 16, 1828. In 1830 he told his brother John (whom he had educated for medicine) that he was writing "a very singular piece. It glances from heaven to earth and back again, in a strange satirical frenzy, whether fine or not remains to be seen." This was "Sartor Resartus."

Mrs. Carlyle wrote that Craigenputtock was not such a frightful place as some folks believed. If cut off from good society she was also delivered from bad. They had horses to ride, and instead of shopping and morning calls, she had bread to bake and chickens to hatch. Carlyle, in a letter to Goethe, which Froude ought to have printed in his "Life," described the place as "among granite hills and the black morasses which stretch through Galloway almost to the Irish Sea. In this wilderness of heath and rock our estate stands forth a green oasis, a tract of ploughed, partly enclosed and planted ground, where corn ripens and trees afford a shade, although surrounded by sea-mews and rough-woolled sheep. Here, with no small effort, have we built and furnished a neat substantial dwelling, where in absence of a professional or other office, we live to cultivate literature according to our strength, and in our own peculiar way. .... This nook of ours, the loneliest in Britain, is six miles from anyone likely to visit us."

Our pictures of Craigenputtock and of Carlyle's study are again from Mr. Napier's photographs. The room has only one window, which looks out into the farm-yard. The grate is the same as in Carlyle's time. Over the mantel, in the frame, is an engraving of Craigenputtock, which Carlyle had done to send to Goethe. Carlyle wrote his essay on Burns in this room; then his essay on Voltaire, and also "Sartor Resartus."

With regard to the general view of Craigenputtock,

Mr. Napier says that the house is very difficult to photograph on account of the trees. Carlyle planted most of these trees himself. The farm buildings are at the back of the house. Carlyle's study, as stated above, was to the back. He built the porch in front. The window on the right of the porch, next to the gate was that of his dining-room. The window on the left of the porch, that of his drawing-room. A door opened off the drawing-room into his study.

Part IV.

CARLYLE IN LONDON.

> *" Here eyes do regard you*
> *In Eternity's stillness;*
> *Here is all fulness,*
> *Ye brave, to reward you.*
> *Work, and despair not !"*
>
> GOETHE (translated by Carlyle).

CHAPTER XI.

MEMORIALS OF CHEYNE ROW, CHELSEA.

From Craigenputtock to Chelsea—Carlyle's word-picture of Cheyne Row—A famous literary workshop—An evening with Tennyson—Some distinguished foreigners—Froude and Ruskin—A glimpse of Mrs. Carlyle—A talk in Carlyle's study—The tragedy of the Carlyle House—Closing scenes.

IN 1834, "the six years' imprisonment," as Froude calls it, "on the Dumfriesshire moor" came to an end, and the Carlyles moved from Craigenputtock to Chelsea, into the house which was to be their home till death. Carlyle had been up in London alone, diligently house-hunting — staying sometimes in rooms previously occupied by Edward Irving, in Woburn Buildings, close to Dickens' home at Tavistock House. At last he pitched on Cheyne Row, attracted thither by the glowing reports of his friend, Leigh Hunt. "The street," wrote Carlyle to his wife, "is flag pathed, small storied, iron railed, all old-fashioned and tightly done up ... The house itself is eminent, antique, wainscoted to the very ceiling, and has been all new painted and repaired; broadish stair with massive balustrade; floor thick as a rock, wood of them here and there worm-eaten, yet capable of cleanness, and still with thrice the strength of a modern floor. And then, as to rooms, Goody! Three stories beside the sunk story, in every one of them three apartments—a front dining-room (marble chimney-piece, &c.), then a back dining-room or breakfast-room; then out of this a china-room or pantry, or I know not what, all shelved, and fit to hold crockery for the whole street. Such is the ground area, which of course continues to the top, and furnishes every bedroom with a dressing-room and second bedroom; on the whole a most massive, roomy, sufficient old house, with places, for example, to hang, say, three dozen hats or cloaks on, and as many crevices and queer old presses and shelved closets as would gratify the most covetous goody—rent £35! I confess I am strongly tempted." And so the house was taken. "Her arrival here I best of all remember. Ah me! She was clear for this poor house (which she gradually, as poverty a little withdrew after long years' pushing, has made so beautiful and comfortable) in preference

CARLYLE'S LONDON LODGINGS, 5, WOBURN BUILDINGS.

to all my other samples; and here we spent our two-and-thirty years of hard battle against fate; hard, but not quite unvictorious, when she left me in her car of

THE STAIRCASE AND GARDEN.

heaven's fire." Thus wrote Carlyle, in his remorseful and most pathetic reminiscences of his deceased Jeannie, of the house No. 5 (now 24), Cheyne Row, to which he and his wife moved in the summer of 1834, from which he sent forth from time to time some of the greatest masterpieces which have enriched English literature in the nineteenth century, and in which he died on February 5, 1881.

THE FRONT ROOM, GROUND FLOOR.

To tell the story of Carlyle's life in Chelsea would be altogether beyond the scope of this book. It is the story of "Carlyle's Life in London (1834–1881)" which Mr. Froude made into two volumes, always of absorbing and often of painful interest. It was here—in No. 5,

CARLYLE'S HOUSE, CHEYNE ROW.

Cheyne Row—the house which is now a permanent memorial of the stormy genius* which once inhabited it—that nearly all the chief works which have made him

BACK ROOM, GROUND FLOOR.

famous were written. At this front door it was that John Stuart Mill knocked one evening in the early spring of 1835, and half staggering up the stairs announced that a careless housemaid had destroyed the

* "What can you say of Carlyle," said Mr. Ruskin to Mr. Froude, "but that he was born in the clouds and struck by the lightning?"

MS. of "The French Revolution." It was from this house that Carlyle trudged forth in search of a publisher for "Sarto Resartus," and from here that he set out to deliver his lectures on "Heroes and Hero Worship." The same house was the workshop in which "Cromwell" and "Frederick" were beaten so laboriously into shape. "It nearly killed me," wrote Carlyle of the latter work. "On Sunday evening in the end of January (1865) I walked out, with the multiplex feeling—joy not very prominent in it, but a kind of solemn thankfulness traceable, that I had written the last sentence of that unutterable book, and, contrary to many forebodings in bad hours, had actually got done with it for ever." An "unutterable book" to Carlyle; and on the face of his wife, who also had endured much during the thirteen years which went to its completion, "there was a silent, faint, and pathetic smile," when the last leaf was at last despatched to the printers. There are not many houses in which so much enduring work has been done as in this literary workshop in Cheyne Row; and the vast amount of biographical matter which has recently been given to the world enables us to enjoy the privilege (if such be the right words for it), in a degree unparalleled in literary history, of feeling the very pulse of the machine and hearing the grinding of the wheels. "I know not," said Carlyle, when he handed to his wife the MS. of the "French Revolution," "whether this book is worth anything, nor what the world will do with it, or misdo, or entirely forbear to do, as is likeliest; but this I could tell the world: you have not had for 100 years any book that comes more direct and flamingly from the heart of a living man."

Here it was, in these same rooms now open to the public, that the Titanic strife of that flaming heart was waged—here that Carlyle (in Mr. Morley's well-known phrase) "compressed the golden 'Gospel of Silence,' in thirty-five volumes," with such dogged tenacity and single-minded devotion, but also at so unutterable an expenditure of fume and fret.

As a literary workshop alone the Carlyle House in Cheyne Row would be of unique interest. But it was here also that the growing fame of its master gathered from time to time all who were most famous in the literature of the Victorian age. Who does not remember Carlyle's description of Tennyson? One evening when he came home from his usual walk, he found the poet sitting in the garden with Mrs. Carlyle, smoking comfortably. "A fine large-featured, dim-eyed, bronze-coloured, shaggy-headed man is Alfred," wrote Carlyle; "dusty, smoky, free and easy, who swims outwardly and inwardly with great composure in an inarticulate element of tranquil chaos and tobacco smoke, great now and then when he does emerge— a

G

most restful, brotherly, solid-hearted man." Another visitor* to Cheyne Row has recorded one such smoking Parliament as Carlyle describes. The Poet Laureate was the other guest. "In the course of conversation they spoke about the difficulty of making speeches; when Tennyson said if allowed to sit he might manage it, but it was severe upon the nerves to stand up when everyone else was sitting. The question was discussed as to whether they would accept titles if offered. Tennyson was disposed to decline such honour for himself, and said no title could excel the simple name of *Thomas Carlyle*. After dinner long clay pipes were laid on the table, and a smoking Parliament commenced." Nor were Carlyle's distinguished visitors confined to his own countrymen. Mazzini (to name one only of his famous foreign visitors) "came much about us" (Carlyle writes), "for many years patronized by my wife—to me very wearisome, with his incoherent Jacobinisms, George Sandism, in spite of all my love and regard for him; a beautiful little man, full of sensibilities, of melodies, of clear intelligence, and noble virtues." Of a very different character was another distinguished foreigner who once crossed Carlyle's threshold, whirling thither "in a chariot that struck all Chelsea into mute amazement with splendour." This

* "Memories of a Long Life," By Lieut.-Col. David Davidson, C.B. (1890).

was none other than "the Phœbus Apollo of Dandyism," Count D'Orsay—"a tall fellow of six feet three, built like a tower, with floods of dark auburn hair, with a beauty, with an adornment unsurpassable on this planet; withal a rather substantial fellow at bottom, by no means without insight, without fun, and a sort of rough sarcasm rather striking out of such a porcelain figure."

Not less interesting is the succession of men who came to this door as disciples to sit at the feet of the Sage of Chelsea. Most famous of these are two great men of letters—one (J. A. Froude) himself recently deceased, the other (John Ruskin) still happily with us. It was in 1849 that Froude made his first pilgrimage to the house in Cheyne Row, where for so many years he was received as a friend, and of whose secrets he was to be made the repository. "James Spedding took me down to Cheyne Row," says Froude, in describing this, his first introduction to Carlyle, "one evening in the middle of June. We found him sitting after dinner, with his pipe, in the small flagged court between the house and the garden. He was then 54 years old; tall (about five feet eleven), thin, but at that time upright, with no signs of the later stoop.... The face was altogether most striking, most impressive every way. And I did not admire him the less because he treated me—I cannot say unkindly, but shortly and sternly. I saw then what I saw ever after—that no one need look for conventional politeness from Carlyle—he would hear the exact truth from him, and nothing else. We went afterwards into the dining-room, where Mrs. Carlyle gave us tea. Her features were not regular, but I thought I had never seen a more interesting-looking woman. Her hair was raven black, her eyes dark, soft, sad, with dangerous light in them. Carlyle's talk was rich, full, and scornful, even delicately mocking." It was some years later that Carlyle made the acquaintance of another young man, whose friendship was very dear to him, and whose discipleship was never to be interrupted. This was Mr. Ruskin, who became a frequent visitor at Cheyne Row, and who, when the little back garden was too hot for Carlyle, was delighted to welcome him at Denmark Hill. "No one," said Mrs. Carlyle, once to a friend,* " managed Carlyle so well as Ruskin ; it was beautiful to see him. Carlyle would say outrageous things, running counter to all Ruskin valued and cared for. Ruskin would treat Mr. Carlyle like a naughty child, lay his arms round him, and say : 'Now, this is too bad!'" Carlyle himself has described an occasion on which in this house " I had Ruskin for some hours, really interesting and entertaining. . . . There is, in singular environment, a ray of real heaven in Ruskin. Passages of his last book, 'Queen of the Air,'

* "Anne Gilchrist : her Life and Writings." (1887) p. 82.

A VIEW OF THE GARDEN AT CHEYNE ROW.

went into my heart like arrows." What talks they must have had! Sometimes Carlyle would sit out alone in the starry night. At other times what conversation, what stores of learning, of eloquence, of wit, and pathos have been poured out when friends such as

THE DRAWING ROOM.

Ruskin, Tennyson, and Froude have sat out among the alder trees, with Herr Teufelsdröckh in the midst of them! And here, too, after the worshipper of Silence had held forth unchecked for two hours or more by the clock, Mrs. Carlyle would pour out some of her brilliant mockery on Mr. Carlyle's "purely platonic love" of that golden divinity! One friend and neighbour—

Alexander Gilchrist, the biographer of William Blake, has given interesting accounts of evenings with "the Sage." Here is one of them:—

"After tea Mrs. Carlyle left, and for the rest of the evening till twelve I sat with him alone, he pouring himself out as is his wont; sitting the latter part of the time on a footstool by the fire, smoking and looking, in his old long brown kind of great coat, as he was bewailing the pass men and things had come to, and as he thought of it, hardly caring to live, looking like a veritable Prophet, mourning in sackcloth and ashes, the sins of the world.... Carlyle took me up into his study, showed his daguerreotype from Cooper's 'Cromwell,' for which he has a great fondness; his screen covered with small portraits relative to Frederick;* a framed

ENTRANCE TO THE STUDY.

* "It was his habit to paste on a screen in his work-room engraved portraits, when no better could be had, of the people he was then writing about. It kept the image of the man steadily in view."—"Conversations with Carlyle. By Sir Charles Gavan Duffy."

Albert Dürer, that had once belonged to the Elector of Saxony, who saved Dante." But to mention all the friends, acquaintances, and disciples who have trod those stairs would require a volume to itself. Leigh Hunt, John Stuart Mill, Erasmus Darwin, Owen, Sterling, Emerson, Harriet Martineau, Frederick Maurice, Thirlwell, Edward Fitzgerald, Kingsley, Spedding, John Bright, Tyndall—these are but a few of the famous men and women, in addition to those referred to already, whose voices these walls have heard. And besides all these, there is the great army of less distinguished pilgrims who came to the home of the Sage of Chelsea for light and leading, for counsel and inspiration, and who, if they came sincerely and modestly, were never sent empty away.

But in these latter days, Carlyle's home in Cheyne Row has been invested with yet another interest—the interest of domestic tragedy. Indeed there are many persons who are well versed in "the Carlyle question," but who have never read a line of Carlyle's books. Nor is this wonderful. The "daily jar and fret" of the Carlyle household has its counterpart, no doubt, in many another house. But in this case both Carlyle and his wife had the gift of literary expression developed to the utmost degree. In Mr. Froude, moreover, they found a biographer who, having convinced himself that his duty was to tell the whole truth, devoted all the resources of his art to making his story interesting and even thrilling. Carlyle's life in London—which is known to us as intimately as Johnson in the pages of Boswell—may be said to pass, in Mr. Froude's pages, through three phases —penury, jealousy, remorse. That, as was said by a reviewer at the time,* was "the grim tragedy of Carlyle's life." Recollections of that tragedy will necessary haunt every visitor to the house which was the scene of so much self-inflicted misery. Perhaps, as a recent critic has observed, the shrewdest, if not the most sympathectic, thing ever said on the subject was Tennyson's remark, that it was well the Carlyles married each other; for had they married differently, there would have been four unhappy persons instead of two.

It would be beyond the scope of this little volume to enlarge on the topics thus suggested. Are they not written in volume after volume of "Carlyleana"? It will be more fitting here, and more in consonance with the impressions one would fain derive from a visit to Carlyle's home, to end our present chapter with the recollection of one of the proudest and then of the saddest moments in its history. From Cheyne Row it was that Carlyle, elected Lord Rector, fared forth in March, 1866, to Edinburgh to deliver his address. It was his

* *Pall Mall Gazette*, October 16, 1884.

last adieu to his Jeannie. "The last I saw of her was as she stood with her back to the parlour door to bid me good-bye. She kissed me twice, she me once, I her a second time." The address was delivered. Professor Tyndall telegraphed to the anxious wife that it was "a perfect triumph." The proud woman read the message exultingly: "the maids of Cheyne Row clapped their hands, and Maggie Welsh danced for delight." Dickens and Wilkie Collins joined Mrs. Carlyle at Forster's house that same evening, and "made good joy" with her over her husband's success. Alas! in a few days (Saturday), April 21, the brave, devoted woman, the loyal-hearted wife of so many years, who had recognised his genius when none else had done so, lay stricken in death, and the Rector of Edinburgh University, whom all the world was now proclaiming "a great man," returned to find her "lying in her coffin, lovely in death."

CHAPTER XII.

A DESECRATED SHRINE.

From sad to mad – The reign of the cats in the Carlyle House —At play with "the darlings" in the garden—An ejectment and the close of this chapter

AFTER the saddest days of the Carlyle House were over, the maddest began. For a time the rooms were empty. Then a maiden lady, as fond of cats and dogs as the Countess de la Torre herself, and almost as much " persecuted " by unkind neighbours and magistrates more unkind, took the house and brought into it a family of some thirty spaniels and cats. This company held the house, and had it all their own way in the garden. The creatures had long learned to live together in peace and unity; also, they were mostly so weary with overfeeding and with great ease and sloth generally,

CAT AND DOG LIFE AT CHEYNE ROW.

that they did not find it in their hearts to quarrel with each other, so long as they each had a sofa, an easy chair, or a soft cushion to repose upon. Only when the horde was sent out into the garden, for hygienic purposes, did they show any spirit. They did not like the open air, and they said so in unmistakable howls and yelps, and caterwaulings. Also, their presence in the garden became otherwise objectionable to the neighbours' senses. And then the occupier of the Carlyle House was summoned to appear before Her Majesty's magistrates. Whenever she did this, she appeared in no wise overawed by the representatives of the law. In fact she represented injured innocence from first to last. Who were those people that thus unwarrantably interfered with the good old British maxim that a man's (or a woman's) house is his castle? Did she interfere with her neighbours' pets? Then let them leave her in peace. Having thus delivered her soul, she paid her fines, and went home to her spaniel-scented domain till another revolting occupant of Cheyne Row had the law on her.

This game went on for some time, and during this period should hero worship or any other motive take you to the Carlyle House, it was difficult indeed to obtain admittance. For money it could not be done, for the lady of the dogs and cats cared not for filthy lucre; but for love you might, if you were very lucky, enter the old sacred portals. Not for the love of man or woman; far from it, for misanthropy goes often hand in hand with the great devotion to unlimited cats and dogs. But if you could make it clear that, "honour bright," you also were addicted to the keeping of pets, and that cats and dogs were your favourite study, you might come in, provided always you were ready with a good deal of sympathy.

Standing on the stone steps in front of the house, and parleying through a mysterious hole in the door, it was easy enough to remain brilliantly eloquent on the beauty of toms, tabbies, and spaniels. But, ye gods! how difficult it was after once you got inside! Even in the narrow hall the air was such that it required heroic stoicism not to fly for dear life. You dared not sit down to recover, for the seats and the carpets were not of the kind on which any ordinary mortal could venture to repose even for a moment. And while you gasped, and hypocritically praised such of the fat, nasty-eyed dogs and "moulting" cats as trundled about, the guardian of these quarters talked to you on the cruelty of magistrates, and the general degeneracy of the public. Max Nordau himself could not have beaten her.

Then you were led into the dining-room, to see more cats and dogs and birds in dirty cages. The air thick with—with what? "Ye winds and waters, say!" The windows coated with dust; the curtains and covers what the sickly monsters had made them; the carpet alive; the "altogether" awful. You dared not, for one moment, think of the serious side of the case; of the temple thus desecrated, or you would have sat down in despair. And sit down you simply dared not. A sick dog growled, and a mangy cat stood on her toes to arch her back the better; otherwise the poor creatures said nothing. Faint, yet pursuing, you mounted the stairs; the drawing-room, bedroom, passages, it was all the same. Words cannot adequately describe it. At last the famous sound-proof room was reached. It was empty, bare, and forgotten, save for some rubbish in a corner. A felt-covered door between the outer and inner wall was opened, and out of the recess came yet another cat, a long thin fellow, blear-eyed, with a coat that may once have been black and smooth, but was all in tatters now, and showed bits of a brownish tint, like worn out furs. The ghastliness of this last scene in the drama was almost too much to stand. "Let us go and look at the garden where the darlings play," you suggested, gathering up the last shreds of hypocrisy at your disposal in the very room where such utter damnation had been pronounced against all shams and humbugs. Into the garden you were shown, for your punishment. It does not do to go into the details of that establishment of damp decay. You soon went back, took in one more whiff of the pestilential air inside, and departed from the Carlye House, a sadder and not a much wiser hero-worshipper.

After a while the horrors of the house became such that the dogs and cats were actually "ordered out," by the authorities. They went to Yarmouth, in detachments, and so this chapter in the history of 5, Cheyne Row, was closed.

CARLYLE'S CHEST OF DRAWERS.

CHAPTER XIII.

THE CARLYLE HOUSE AS IT IS.

Honour to the great dead—American worshippers to the shrine
—A walk round the house—"If the furniture had tongue"
—Carlyle's books and book-plate—The Carlyle relics.

IT seemed worth while to describe the episode in the history of Carlyle's house, dealt with in the last chapter, if only to make the reader appreciate the more the rescue which has now been achieved. The house in which Carlyle lived for fifty years is now out of danger; and at last London will have a shrine to which literary pilgrims may repair for a little hero worship. Hitherto we have left the work of commemorating the houses of famous Londoners to a small society, the result of whose efforts may be seen in a few smoky tablets, which are dotted about here and there. So to have actually secured a whole house; to have bought it outright; to have acquired the beginnings of a museum; to have paid a caretaker to show us round— is indeed an unheard of advance in our desire to do honour to the great dead. Some day we may even find time and money to do the same for a Hogarth or Turner, an Addison, a Thackeray, a Dickens, a Charles Lamb, a Goldsmith, a Johnson, a Tennyson, or even a Walpole or a Gladstone. But we dare only whisper this, for the controversy which has raged round this modest Chelsea scheme bids us be very careful in assuming any such fantastic suggestions for the present. Some very excellent judges, for instance, objected to any memorial to Carlyle because of his abominable style; others, because of numerous apostrophes to Sun, and Moon and Stars; others, because no one can read Carlyle; but the great objection, and the one that nearly proved fatal, was because he quarrelled with his wife, *and all the world knew it!* Yet, if those revelations had only been withheld by that wicked Mr. Froude, it would have been a different matter; and they might have done what they liked. But a man who quarrelled with his wife—and made no secret of it—was no fellow to make a fuss about. He was a man of genius (and she a woman not without brains) who should have known better. How these objections were met will never be known; somehow or other they were overcome, and No. 24 is swept and furnished from cellar to garret, and for the modest sum of one shilling every admirer of Carlyle has the right of entry.

No less than sixteen hundred visitors paid their shillings during the first three months that the house was thrown open to the public. Of these about a third are Americans; the others being Britons. These ladies and gentlemen have taken the keenest interest in every room in the house; so much, indeed, that the caretaker, Mrs. Strong, has often had the greatest difficulty in persuading them to move on. There are stories of American ladies who have sat down in Carlyle's study chair for an hour at a time, seeking inspiration, we may suppose. Many of the visitors—especially those ardent Americans—have indited letters to their bosom friends proudly dated: "Carlyle House." Indeed, so greatly did Mr. Blunt (the honorary secretary to whom we are indebted for much of the information that appears in this chapter) fear that no chairs would be left at all if some preventive measures were not taken, that he has placed stout pieces of string across every chair now, so that sentimental pilgrims must fain stand. Then again, many of the visitors, especially those from across the Atlantic, begged for a leaf from the shrubs in the garden, a brick from the three hundred-year-old wall, and some of them it is believed, took away a pocketful of earth.

But we will now turn showmen and escort you round the house, which was built by Lord Cheyne in 1701.

MRS. CARLYLE'S FIRE-SCREEN.

It is none of your modern jerry-built dwellings, but a stout, solid, John Bull sort of a house, which will be as good in another century as it is to-day. Carlyle himself used this fact to point more than one moral; and the bricks of his garden wall are mentioned in one of the pamphlets — "Shooting Niagara," is it not? They are *three* hundred years of age, and still in admirable preservation, though a little going. The very door, with its sombre black iron knocker, has a defiant look about it, its back being especially noteworthy. So don't forget to look at it; and lift the great chain—if you can—the end of which drops into an iron spiral. No burglar

THE FRONT DOOR.

could ever saw it through. The hall itself is narrow, dark, and covered with some deep mahogany paper, which is carried up the staircases to the very top of the house. On the left is the dining-room in which you will ultimately pause for a few minutes. There is no carpet on the floor at present, though when funds are more plentiful they will doubtless weave a special carpet, which shall be as near a match to the real article as loom, wool, and dyer are able to produce. But that modest round table there, in the centre, is the veritable

The Dining Table

dining table, a rather frail thing of mahogany, which divides into two by some ingenious contrivance. You will look at this piece of furniture with respect, not unmixed with a certain awe, for it has doubtless witnessed some stormy scenes. You can imagine Carlyle coming down to breakfast in a mighty ill-humour; those breakfasts at No. 24 must have been awful meals. The cocks have kept him awake all night, or the porridge is not to his liking, or it is too hot, or too cold—the whole world is against him. Mrs. Carlyle's slumbers, perhaps, have not been too restful. She, too, has heard those cocks crowing; they began at midnight, the industrious birds; then, maybe, there was a little bill to pay, and she daren't ask Carlyle for money. So, doubtless, *she* was not in too good a humour. And such was the beginning of a pleasant day! Or, if it was not the cook, the egg which the great man took after his porridge was not quite above suspicion. It was from the little shop round the corner, and Mrs. Carlyle looks slyly to see if her lord and master will find it out. Happily, his thoughts are far away in red fool-fury, fighting with Frederick or Cromwell, or elsewhere. So the egg passes muster, and off he marches upstairs for the rest of the day. But you can talk to the table yourself; write a letter on it if you like; or at least inscribe your name in the big visitors' book which now rests upon it. The first thing you had best do when you enter is to look for a moment at Mrs. Allingham's little pencil sketches which hang over the mantelpiece. A day or two after Carlyle died, this delightful artist, who was an intimate friend, called and made sketches of each of the rooms, and of the staircases, and the garden. Thus, happily, we can form a very accurate picture of each of the rooms as it was when the Carlyles were alive. In those days the folding-doors were closed, and a large bookcase hid them. At present this table is the chief object of interest, but in time there is little doubt that most of

CARLYLE ON FRITZ.

the furniture will be replaced. In one corner is the plaster mask of Carlyle taken by the late Mr. Boehm two or three days after his death. The flesh is much shrunken, and the nose is as aquiline as the Iron Duke's. This has been lent by the Rector of Chelsea. On the mantelpiece are a pair of silvergilt candlesticks; and on the wall above hangs an excellent picture of Carlyle on his famous horse Fritz—a short, cobby, good-looking animal. It is an enlargement of a photograph taken by Mr. G. G. Napier, who has kindly allowed it to be reproduced in these pages. Do not forget to look at the fireplace, which was recovered from beneath a heap of iron scrap in the north of London; a fender and fire-irons are the original articles.

— CARLYLE'S INK STAND —

— SILVER CANDLESTICK —

Now let us into the dark little back dining-room with a small window looking into the garden. Here you will see one of the bookcases—a very humble affair of painted deal; but full of Carlyle's books. And a very shabby lot they are—very dusty, leaving signs of hard usage, and intrinsically worth about twopence each; old-fashioned dictionaries, geographies, peerages, odd volumes of Goethe, Schiller, Grimm,

Schlegel, Bohn's translations, and so on. Many o them contain marginal notes in Carlyle's writing, and in most of them you will find the Carlyle book plate, with its motto: "Humiliate." Against the wall is his old red sofa, rather hard, but room enough, which used to be kept at the foot of his bed upstairs. At the end of the room in a tiny closet, in the corner of which is a little wooden bracket, one of Mrs. Carlyle's household treasures. Each of these bits of furniture which we have mentioned bears signs of most careful usage. That household was, as we all know, administered with an attention to *minutiæ* which is most pathetic. But money was very scarce at No. 24 for many a bitter year, and the tragedy is writ large on each of these bits of china and sticks of furniture.

SOFA IN THE DINING ROOM.

And now to the garden, in which you must certainly remain for a few minutes. It is not at all a bad garden for a London house which was rented at £35 a year. Here Carlyle, when he wanted a little exercise, or was a little more bilious and irritable than usual, worked off the travelling acids and evil humours, "delved to compose himself," or "stayed smoking in the back court" through the June night, "till the great dawn streamed up" before his eyes. Many of those fine apostrophes to sun and moon must have been inspired by such glimpses of those bodies as he got from this sooty little garden, with its patch of grass or gravel path. Under the ash tree he and Tennyson smoked

ONE OF CARLYLE'S BOOK-CASES.

many a pipe together; and other famous men, no doubt. And that is the famous wall at the end there. In the early days it was not quite so overlooked as it is now— by laundries and schools. That sea-green bit of china —how to describe it we know not—was Carlyle's; and in the summer he had an awning stretched over him, beneath which he sat and worked, or thought and smoked.

Do not despise the kitchen, which is down below.

It is like most kitchens, though the fittings are old-fashioned. There is a pump in the corner, for instance, and the great fire-place is made smaller or larger by a lever; and from the chimney swings a great hook on which

THE KITCHEN.

the pots were placed. Many a time has Mrs. Carlyle leant over it. Here she made the famous marmalade, "pure as liquid amber, in taste and in look almost poetically delicate;" and here Leigh Hunt's "endlessly admirable morsel of Scotch porridge" was stirred at

CARLYLE'S GARDEN.

the evening's close. On that mantel stood, in early years, the tinder-box to which Carlyle had often groped his way, when the sleepless night became insufferable, to find flint and steel for his pipe. We give on page 128 a little sketch which is a faithful representation of it. The table and dresser are the original articles

and on the shelf there you will see three or four pieces of the Carlyle dinner service. Here is the pattern.

Now mount the steps again, and, having climbed up the staircase—note the spiral balusters of dark pitch-pine—enter the drawing-room, which is so often described in the letters, "the room she gradually made so beautiful and comfortable," the "warm little parlour," where Carlyle and his wife "sat snug most evenings in stuffed chairs." It is a very pleasant room, well lighted by three windows. Again you will just glance at Mrs. Allingham's sketches; then look at the

ANOTHER OF CARLYLE'S BOOK-CASES.

book-case, of the same pattern as the one downstairs, and full of books. One-half is nearly filled by an ancient set of "Annual Registers;" the other is a shabby and miscellaneous collection. It would never do to allow visitors to turn them over—this is protected by glass

MRS. CARLYLE.

doors, and the one below has been wired over—but Mr. Blunt kindly opens a few of them for us. One we noticed—a copy of "The Earthly Paradise"—was a gift from Mr. Ruskin to Carlyle "from his scholar, with love." The lower half is made into cupboards, which are full of Voltaire's works—ninety-seven volumes, we believe! There is little else to be seen but pictures: a fragile table, and a faded Oriental screen. But this was the best known room in the house; in which some of the most famous men and women of the day had taken tea with the Carlyles, and discussed every subject under the sun. And there, by the fireplace, is the spot where Carlyle used to sit on the rug, "his back against the mantel-jamb, his wife reclining on the sofa, a bright, kindly fire, candles hardly lit, all in trustful chiaroscuro, with a pipe of tobacco, and door never so little open, so that all the smoke went up the chimney."

So regard it with veneration. In the corner there by the window Carlyle died; through the folding-door is Mrs. Carlyle's bedroom—empty it is now—whither she was borne on that memorable day when she was found lifeless in her carriage, and Carlyle was away giving his rectorial address to the Edinburgh students. Now, upstairs to see the most famous room in the house, namely, that sound-proof study which Carlyle built on the roof-tops, at a cost of £200, in 1853. It is like a studio to all intents and purposes; lighted by a big window above. "The sublime garret, double-doored, double-windowed, impervious to snow." It is, indeed, an uncomfortable-looking room, but here

THE SOUND-PROOF ROOM.

Carlyle wrote that terrible "Frederic." Portraits of that famous warrior and statesman still hang on the wall, next to one of his friend Voltaire. Very shaky

THOMAS CARLYLE, ABOUT 1850.
(From a photograph by the London Stereoscopic Company.)

very grimy they look now, as do those two maps of Ireland and Scotland. The only article of furniture here at present is the chair which Carlyle used when at work—an affair of black horse-hair, with arms—which

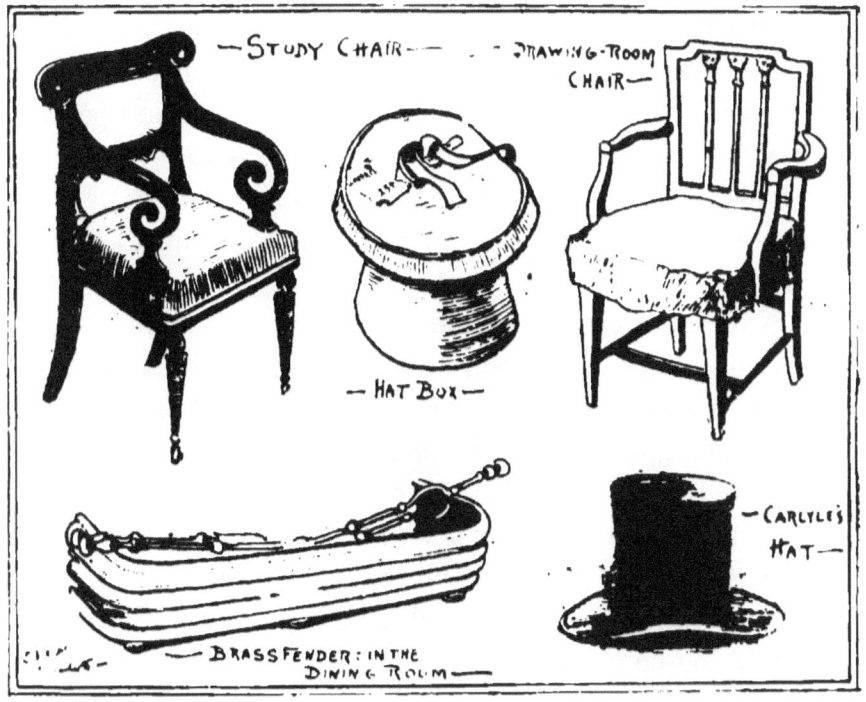

looks easy enough, and in very good preservation. The desk on which he wrote each one of his thirty or fifty volumes is now in the possession of Lady Fitzjames Stephen. We need not repeat the well-known story of the room—"most entirely detestable and despicable piece of workmanship," which Carlyle soon found was anything but sound-proof. He must have conquered his dislike to it for some years, though after "Frederic" was written he generally worked in the drawing-room. In the winter it was too cold; in the summer it was too hot; and in the windy weather the soot covered the floor. The legend runs that one day he was found sousing the deposit with a watering-pot! His fondness for fresh air could be guessed by the remarkable number of ventilators which are to be seen above the home: in the garret alone the number was ten!

Now step downstairs again, and look at Carlyle's bed —a four-poster, hung with red curtains. There is his chest of drawers; and in the little closet his hip bath, his washing stand, a beaver hat of enormous dimensions (which now stands under a glass-case to prevent the visitors from trying it on), his hat-box, and his stick.

And that is all for the present, but it is hoped that some of the remarkable relics which were lent for exhibition on the occasion of the centenary of his birth, will be allowed to remain at No. 24.

CARLYLE'S BED.

CONCLUSION.

" It is an old belief
 That on some solemn shore,
Beyond the sphere of grief,
 Dear friends shall meet once more:

Beyond the sphere of time,
 And sin and fate's control,
Serene in changeless prime
 Of body and of soul.

That creed I fain would keep,
 This hope I'll not forego:
Eternal be the sleep,
 If not to waken so."

Verses of Lockhart's "often on Carlyle's lips" (Froude's "Carlyle's Life in London," i. 250).

A VISIT TO CARLYLE'S GRAVE.

As is too common with us, a poor minimum of care seems to be bestowed upon the God's acre where Carlyle and his kindred lie quiet in death. Surrounded by a rude and bare stone wall, entered through an unlovely iron gate, the graves in general speak eloquently of the forgetfulness of human sorrow.

The Carlyle grave is an exception to this rule: inside the high iron railing that surrounds it, perpetuating the Carlyle aloofness even in death, the grass is closely cut, and daisies are the only weeds allowed to grow there. There are three graves within the enclosure, Carlyle being buried in the centre. In the grave to the left sleep his father and mother and two of his sisters; also his father's wife by his first marriage. Carlyle's reminiscences of his father and the reflections which he entered in his journal on his mother's death, prove what a wealth of affection he bore towards his parents.

The grave to the right is that of Carlyle's brother James, of whom many characteristic and even Carlylean stories were told us. To a certain extent he appears to have shared the old roadman's opinions of his famous brother's work, or, at the least, to have been indifferent to immortal achievements in the realm of literature.

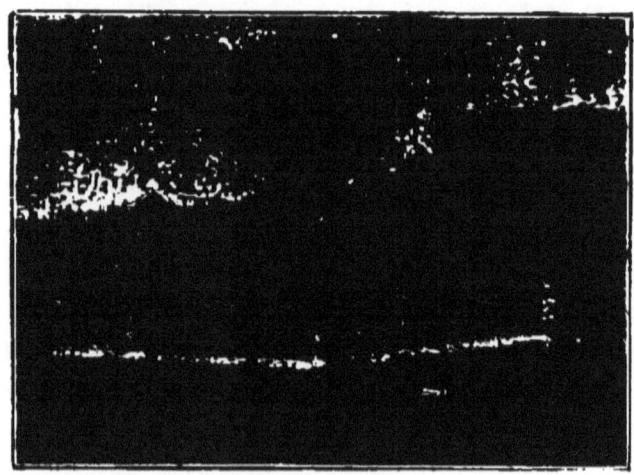

THE CARLYLE LAIR: ECCLEFECHAN.

He was met one day in the village by a party of American pilgrims, who, ignorant of his identity, asked of him the whereabouts of Carlyle's grave. "Which Carlyle?" "Oh, the great Carlyle, Thomas Carlyle." With unmoved face he gave the information asked, and was rewarded with a fine outburst of hero-worship. "We have come all the way from America," said the spokesman of the pilgrims, "to lay this wreath on our great teacher's grave." "Hah!" rejoined he, still unmoved,

CARLYLE'S GRAVE.

"it's a gey harmless occupation." Again, at some meeting of the farmers in the district—the rent-day, probably—a dinner was given, and some long-winded yeoman said grace before the meal. Jamie listened throughout it patiently; then saluted his over-devout neighbour with the remark: "A verra guid blessing, Wullie, but ye've spoilt the soup."

No lies are told on Carlyle's tombstone. The inscription is simple and laconic. The family crest: two wyverns, the family motto: *Humilitate*, and then these few words:—

HERE RESTS THOMAS CARLYLE, WHO WAS BORN AT ECCLEFECHAN, 4TH DECEMBER, 1795, AND DIED AT 24, CHEYNE ROW, CHELSEA, LONDON, ON SATURDAY, 5TH FEBRUARY, 1881.

That is all. And yet it is enough. There are two significant, pregnant words—*Humilitate*, "Rests."

www.ingramcontent.com/pod-product-compliance
Lightning Source LLC
Chambersburg PA
CBHW030252170426
43202CB00009B/719